Criminal Justice

Recent Scholarship

Edited by
Marilyn McShane and Frank P. Williams III

A Series from LFB Scholarly

Neighborhood Structure, Crime, and Fear of Crime

Testing Bursik and Grasmick's
Neighborhood Control Theory

Clete Snell

LFB Scholarly Publishing LLC
New York 2001

Copyright © 2001 by LFB Scholarly Publishing LLC

Library of Congress Cataloging-in-Publication Data

Snell, Clete.
  Neighborhood structure, crime, and fear of crime : testing
Bursik and Grasmick's neighborhood control theory / Clete Snell.
    p. cm. -- (Criminal justice recent scholarship)
Includes bibliographical references and index.
  ISBN 1-931202-07-9 (alk. paper)
  1. Sociology, Urban--Research. 2. Social control. 3. Social
networks. 4. Crime. 5. Fear of crime. I. Title. II. Series.
  HT110 .S64 2001
  307.76'072--dc21

2001002453

ISBN 1-931202-07-9

Printed on acid-free 250-year-life paper.

Manufactured in the United States of America.

Table of Contents

Acknowledgements

This book was developed from my doctoral dissertation while at Sam Houston State University. I am grateful to the College of Criminal Justice at SHSU for all I have received while I was there. I am especially grateful to Margaret Farnworth for agreeing to chair my dissertation and Ruth Triplett for all her guidance during my doctoral career. Finally, I want to thank Marilyn McShane for her helpful suggestions in the completion of this book.

CHAPTER 1

Introduction

Over fifty years ago, Clifford Shaw and Henry McKay made one of the most important insights in the field of criminology. High rates of crime and delinquency can persist in certain neighborhoods despite complete turnovers of the racial and ethnic population (Shaw and McKay, 1942). This led Shaw and McKay to the conclusion that delinquency could not be adequately explained by characteristics associated with individuals such as race, ethnicity, nationality, and intelligence. Rather delinquency was intimately associated with the characteristics of particular neighborhoods.

Despite the influence of Shaw and McKay on the field of criminology for many years, the discipline had shifted its focus back toward individual-level explanations of delinquency throughout much of the 1970's and 80's. Only in recent years have "kinds of places" or contextual (Stark, 1996, p. 128) explanations become accepted again (Sampson, 1997).

In "*Neighborhoods and Crime: The Dimensions of Effective Community Control*" (1993), Bursik and Grasmick proposed a "systemic theory of neighborhood control." Their theory is a reformulation of a social disorganization model. The central thesis of Bursik and Grasmick's theory is that differences in neighborhood crime, victimization, and fear of crime can be explained best by variations in the abilities of neighborhoods to regulate and control the behavior of their residents.

The primary purpose of this research was to conduct a partial test of Bursik and Grasmick's theory. This test was conducted using data from the "Crime Changes in Baltimore" study conducted by Ralph Taylor (1998). Taylor collected data to examine the relationship of crime rates and fear of crime with resident's attitudes, physical deterioration, and neighborhood structure in a sample of urban Baltimore neighborhoods.

The purpose and significance of this book are described in the remainder of this chapter. Chapter 2 presents Bursik and Grasmick's theoretical model, propositions and hypotheses from the theory, and conceptual definitions. Chapter 3 reviews the literature concerning the theoretical and empirical relevance of their theoretical model. Chapter 4 presents the research methodology utilized in this book. The final two chapters describe the analyzed results (Chapter 5) and the implications of this research and its findings (Chapter 6).

OBJECTIVES OF THE STUDY

The primary purpose of this study was to conduct a test of Bursik and Grasmick's systemic theory of neighborhood crime control. As previously stated, propositions and hypotheses from their theoretical model were tested using Taylor's "Crime Changes in Baltimore" data. This data has many unique features well suited to test ecological theories and this theory in particular.

This study is important for several reasons. First, Shaw and McKay (1969) were among the first criminologists to identify a relationship between ecologically disadvantaged neighborhoods and crime rates. However, their explanation for the process of *why* neighborhoods are important for understanding crime has been challenged.

Shaw and McKay draw freely on elements of strain, cultural conflict, and control theories (see Kornhauser, 1978), but they fail to integrate propositions from these perspectives in a theoretically meaningful way. Bursik and Grasmick's (1993) theory avoids this problem by explicating how the concepts of social structure, disorder, primary and secondary networks, and neighborhood social control are interrelated.

Thus, Bursik and Grasmick's theory has the promise of explaining the mechanisms by which neighborhoods influence crime. This is a critical issue, for the mere correlation of crime rates with ecological variables is consistent with several criminological theories (Sampson, 1992). In order to go beyond the research of Shaw and McKay, theoretical models detailing the social processes mediating social structure and crime are necessary. This is why Elliott et al. (1996) believe that in many respects the theoretical and empirical discussion of neighborhood effects is still at a rudimentary level.

A second rationale for this research is that tests of two different dependent variables are conducted, crime rates and fear of crime, with the same theoretical model. If both crime and fear of crime can be predicted using the same theory it could lead to consistency in explaining the objective (crime rates) and subjective (fear of crime) aspects of the crime problem.

Third, with this research I conduct a test of a relatively new, important theory that has not yet been fully tested. One reservation about any new theory is its lack of empirical testing and support. Testability and fitting the empirical evidence are two crucial criteria for theory assessment (Akers, 1994).

Finally, this book utilizes two different statistical techniques, Ordinary Least Squares Regression (OLS) and Hierarchical Linear Analysis, to test the same theoretical model. This has the potential to contribute to the statistical debate concerning the better method to test neighborhood or community-level theories. Regression models have been used traditionally in neighborhood-level studies. However, OLS is limited to one unit of analysis. With hierarchical linear analysis, models with two or three levels of analysis can be tested. The method also allows for an understanding of neighborhood versus individual effects.

CHAPTER 2

Bursik And Grasmick's Systemic Theory Of Neighborhood Control

THE THEORETICAL MODEL

Bursik and Grasmick (1993) assert that neighborhood capacity for self-regulation is determined by the extensiveness and density of the formal and informal networks within the neighborhood that bind the residents together. They argue that:

> "the differential rates of criminal behavior and victimization among neighborhoods, and the resulting fear of crime that may develop among the residents of crime-ridden areas, represent variations in the ability of neighborhoods to regulate themselves through these networks in such a way that the daily lives of their residents are not significantly constrained by the threat of criminal behavior" (p. 4).

The previous statement makes it clear that Bursik and Grasmick's theory is a neighborhood control theory. That is, the density and quality of formal and informal networks lead to effective neighborhood social control. Additionally, the above statement makes it clear that Bursik and Grasmick intend that their theory explain not only crime rates, but also victimization and fear of crime.

Bursik and Grasmick present a "basic systemic model of crime" that includes neighborhood social structure, primary and secondary relationships, neighborhood social control, and crime rates (see Figure 1). However, they clearly extend their theory to include several other concepts from the neighborhood and crime literature in recent years.

They devote an entire chapter to fear of crime, discussing conceptual and measurement problems and how previous fear of crime models relate to their own systemic theory. Bursik and Grasmick also discuss how disorder fits into their model. Disorder is an intervening variable in the theory, placed between neighborhood structure and primary and secondary relationships. Disorder is theorized to be a key explanatory variable for fear of crime. These concepts were added to Bursik and Grasmick's basic systemic model in this study (see Figure 2).[1]

As previously mentioned, victimization is a dependent variable in Bursik and Grasmick's theory. It will not be included as a dependent variable in this study due to data limitations. Thus, crime rates and fear of crime are the dependent variables that will be tested in this study.

The Bursik and Grasmick (1993) theoretical model begins with a restatement of Shaw and McKay's (1942) central findings. Neighborhoods characterized by economic deprivation tend to have rates of high population turnover

---

[1] There are other extensions to the model presented by Bursik and Grasmick (e.g., changing ecological structures and opportunity structures). These other extensions were not included due to a desire to maintain a rather parsimonious model and because of a limited sample size.

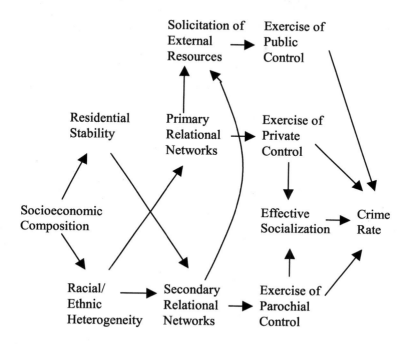

Figure 1. Bursik and Grasmick's Basic Systemic Model of Crime (From "Neighborhoods and Crime: The Dimensions of Effective Community Control)

because they were considered undesirable places to live and people would abandon them at the first opportunity.

Also, this rapid compositional change made it difficult for these communities to resist the influx of incoming groups of people. Poor neighborhoods also tend to be characterized by racial and ethnic heterogeneity.

Shaw and McKay argued that these characteristics made it difficult for neighborhoods to achieve the common goals of its residents. These neighborhoods were socially disorganized. However, the causal link between social disorganization and delinquency was not clearly specified (Kornhauser, 1978; Bursik, 1988).

Bursik and Grasmick extend the social disorganization argument by stating that rapid population turnover and heterogeneity can decrease the ability of a neighborhood to control itself because:

1. "Institutions pertaining to internal control are difficult to establish when many residents are uninterested in communities they hope to leave at the first opportunity.
2. The development of primary relationships that result in informal structures of neighborhood control is less likely when local networks are in a continual state of flux.
3. Heterogeneity impedes communication and thus obstructs the quest to solve common problems and attain common goals" (Bursik and Grasmick, 1993, p. 33).

Bursik and Grasmick propose that instability and the heterogeneity of neighborhoods affect three levels of social control. Bursik and Grasmick rely on Hunter's (1985) description of three levels of direct controls.

The private level refers to relationships among friends. Friends may withdraw esteem, sentiment, and social support in efforts to control other's actions.

The parochial level of control points to the broader set of local interpersonal networks of neighbors, and interlocking of local institutions, such as voluntary organizations, stores, schools, and churches.

The public level of control involves the ability of a community to obtain public goods and services (e.g., health services, social services, policing, etc.) from agencies outside the local community.

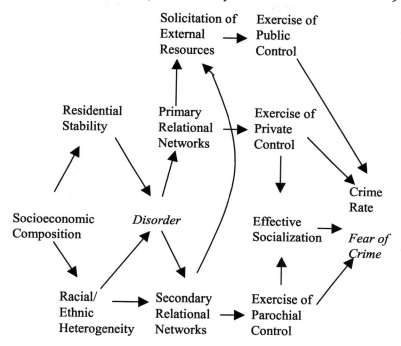

Figure 2. Modification of Bursik and Grasmick's Systemic Model[2]

---

[2] This model was adapted from Bursik and Grasmick's Basic Systemic Model. It is an exact replication of the model displayed on page 39 of Neighborhoods and Crime: The Dimensions of Effective Community Control, except that the concepts fear of crime and disorder were not represented in that original model. Those concepts are extensions of the basic systemic model and of interest in this research.

At the private level, ongoing changes in the residential population of a neighborhood make it very difficult to establish and maintain intimate primary ties within the community. Thus, affective relational networks tend to be fairly superficial and transitory, making the threatened withdrawal of sentiment, support, and esteem a relatively ineffective control. While neighborhood instability makes the development of deep and lasting relational networks difficult, racial and ethnic heterogeneity limit the breadth of relational networks.

At the parochial level, crime control reflects the ability of neighborhoods to supervise the behavior of their residents. Instability and heterogeneity also weaken the supervisory capabilities of these parochial networks.

Greenberg et al. (1982) found that residents are not likely to intercede in criminal events that involve strangers and are reluctant to assume responsibility for the welfare of property that belongs to people they barely know.

The social boundaries that may exist between groups in heterogeneous neighborhoods can also decrease the breadth of supervisory activities due to the mutual distrust among groups in such areas. Thus, racial and ethnic heterogeneity may lead to a differential capacity of neighborhoods to exert parochial control.

Another important component of community self-regulation involves the effectiveness of socialization in preventing deviance. Sampson (1986a, 1987) has argued that parents often take on the responsibility for the behavior of youth other than their own children in relatively stable neighborhoods.

The likelihood of effective socialization and supervision is reduced in communities characterized by residential instability, heterogeneity, and a high proportion of broken and/or single parent families. Cohesive family structures are effective sources of control "because they are aware of and intervene in group activities ... that are usually the predecessors of involvement in more serious delinquent activities" (Sampson, 1987: 107).

Bursik and Grasmick suggest that the greatest shortcoming of the basic social disorganization model is a failure to consider the relational networks that pertain to the public sphere of control. They point to several studies that document the existence of stable neighborhoods with extensive interpersonal networks that nevertheless have relatively high rates of crime and delinquency (Whyte, 1981; Moore, 1978; and Horowitz, 1983). The existence of such neighborhoods is an important contradiction of the predictions of traditional social disorganization approaches, which have focused only on the mutual linkages of residents.

Bursik and Grasmick note that it is difficult to significantly affect the nature of neighborhood life through the efforts of local community organizations alone. Rather, these groups must be able to negotiate effectively with those agencies that make decisions relating to the investment of resources in neighborhoods.

They conclude that the existence of stable, high-crime neighborhoods in itself does not call the validity of the systemic model into question. Rather, it emphasizes the need to expand the focus of control beyond the internal dynamics of the community.

Fear of Crime

Bursik and Grasmick (1993) claim that their systemic neighborhood control model can be applied to fear of crime. They discuss three common fear of crime models that appear in the literature: the indirect victimization model, the neighborhood disorder model, and the heterogeneity model.[3]

While Bursik and Grasmick agree that there is empirical support for the indirect victimization model, they suggest that fear of crime can best be explained by combining the other two models. They use these two models to support their contention that their systemic theory can be utilized to explain fear of crime.[4]

Disorder and Systemic Control

After presenting the basic systemic model, Bursik and Grasmick discuss extensions to the model from recent criminological research.   The first extension that they discuss is disorder, a concept that has developed out of the fear of crime literature (Bursik and Grasmick, 1993).

First of all, Bursik and Grasmick discuss the problem of defining disorder. Wesley Skogan (1990:4) "defines disorder as a violation of norms concerning public behavior." Lewis and Salem (1986: xiv) define the concept as "reflections of the erosion of commonly accepted standards and values".

It generally refers to the presence of graffiti, loitering teens, abandoned and boarded-up buildings, trash strewn vacant lots, public drunkenness, and physically deteriorated housing. Thus, the concept is a much broader normative conceptualization than crime, given rise to the argument that middle-class values are being applied to behavior that many do not find especially problematic.

---

[3] The fear of crime models discussed are not to be confused with either of the models presented in figure 1 or 2. They are competing models of fear of crime presented in past research.

[4] A review of these models is provided in chapter 3 of this book.

However, Lewis and Salem (1986) suggest that middle-class bias may not be as serious a problem as one might expect. They found that while perceptions of disorder varied extensively from neighborhood to neighborhood, there was a great deal of within-neighborhood consensus concerning the distribution of disorder.

Disorder became a salient topic after Wilson and Kelling (1982) argued that disorder can lead directly to crime. They claim that once symbols of disorder become widespread in a neighborhood, behaviors such as vandalism are much more likely because it suggests that nobody cares.

However, Bursik and Grasmick, clearly believe that disorder has a much more important indirect effect on crime. They point to Skogan's (1990) argument that once indicators of social disorder, (such as public drinking, the presence of loitering youths, visible drug and alcohol users, and panhandlers), or physical disorder, (such as abandoned buildings or graffiti), become highly visible in a neighborhood, residents often feel demoralized, helpless and angry.

Skogan's (1990) findings can be directly linked to Bursik and Grasmick's systemic model of neighborhood control. First, while the distribution of disorder is related to the level of poverty, racial composition, and degree of instability in a neighborhood, instability has the greatest effect. Second, high levels of disorder tend to be associated with lowered rates of mutual helping behavior among residents, satisfaction with the area, and stated plans to remain in the neighborhood.

Thus, disorder can seriously disrupt the relational networks within a community, thereby decreasing its ability to control the behavior of its residents. Disorder has been most clearly associated with the fear of crime literature and has been incorporated into victimization models. Bursik and Grasmick (1993) point out that it has yet to be incorporated into systemic models, despite empirical evidence that highlights its relevance (Sampson and Groves, 1989; Gottfredson and Taylor, 1986).

PROPOSITIONS AND HYPOTHESES

While there are many different propositions and hypotheses that can be derived from the systemic control theory, a select number have been developed to test with the available data. Below are two sets of propositions and hypotheses concerning the systemic theory of crime rates and fear of crime.

Hypotheses Concerning the Systemic Model of Crime Rates

Proposition 1: Neighborhood structure characteristics have an indirect effect on crime rates through neighborhood interaction and social control (See Figure 3).

Hypothesis 1: Neighborhoods that are unstable, of low socioeconomic status and racially heterogeneous have weak primary relationships, which in turn increases the crime rate.

Hypothesis 2: Neighborhoods that are unstable, of low socioeconomic status and racially heterogeneous have weak secondary relationships, which in turn increases the crime rate.

Hypothesis 3: Neighborhoods that are unstable, of low socioeconomic status and racially heterogeneous are unable to exercise public control, which in turn increases the crime rate.

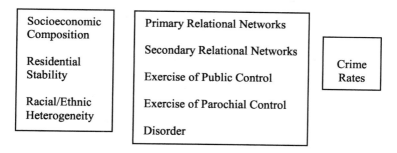

Figure 3. Research Model on Crime Rates based on Bursik and Grasmick's Systemic Theory

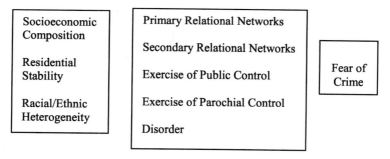

Figure 4. Research Model on Fear of Crime based on Bursik and Grasmick's Systemic Theory[5]

---

[5] From an examination of Figure 1 it is clear that the above set of hypotheses are not an exhaustive list derived from the theoretical model and many causal relationships were not represented. This is a general reflection of the available data and not the theory itself.

Bursik and Grasmick's theory makes predictions concerning the temporal order of the intervening variables. For example, neighborhoods with a disadvantaged socioeconomic position leads to residential instability, which in turn effects primary relationships, thereby increasing the exercise of private control and increasing crime rates. The "Crime Changes in Baltimore" data do not allow for a test of such a hypothesis.

Hypothesis 4: Neighborhoods that are unstable, of low socioeconomic status and racially heterogeneous are unable to exercise parochial control, which in turn increases the crime rate.

Hypothesis 5: Neighborhoods that are unstable, of low socioeconomic status and racially heterogeneous have high levels of disorder, which in turn increases the crime rate.

Hypotheses Concerning the Systemic Model of Fear of Crime

Proposition 1: Neighborhood structure characteristics have an indirect effect on fear of crime through neighborhood interaction and social control (See Figure 4).

Hypothesis 1: Neighborhoods that are unstable, of low socioeconomic status and racially heterogeneous have weak primary relationships, which in turn increases the fear of crime.

Hypothesis 2: Neighborhoods that are unstable, of low socioeconomic status, and racially heterogeneous have weak secondary relationships, which in turn increases the fear of crime.

Hypothesis 3: Neighborhoods that are unstable, of low socioeconomic status and racially heterogeneous are unable to exercise public control, which in turn increases the fear of crime.

Hypothesis 4: Neighborhoods that are unstable, of low socioeconomic status and racially heterogeneous are unable to exercise parochial control, which in turn increases the fear of crime.

Hypothesis 5: Neighborhoods that are unstable, of low socioeconomic status and racially heterogeneous have high levels of disorder, which in turn increases the fear of crime.

DEFINITION OF CONCEPTS

Bursik and Grasmick discuss the concept of neighborhood and various definitions of neighborhood previously used. However, they base their definition of neighborhood on definitions provided by Hunter and Suttles (1972). Hunter and Suttles state that neighborhood residents live within a "pyramid of progressively more inclusive groupings" (p. 45).

The smallest, termed the face-block level, represent a network of acquaintanceship based simply on the propinquity of residence and the common use of local facilities. This neighborhood is embedded within a nominal community, which is the smallest entity with a name known and recognized by both its residents and outsiders (see Table 1).

Bursik and Grasmick state that the dynamics of their theory are assumed to operate at these two levels. The "Crime Changes in Baltimore" data have operationalized neighborhoods at a level consistent with the nominal definition provided above. Socioeconomic composition refers to the economic structure of the neighborhood; the amount of poverty, home values, income levels, and occupational status of residents.

Bursik and Grasmick's (1993) theory states that low-income neighborhoods are generally less attractive to residents leading to residential instability. Low-income neighborhoods contain high levels of minorities because this population is least capable of leaving.

Residential stability refers to the amount of change in the population level of a neighborhood. Bursik and Grasmick argue that ongoing changes in the residential

Table 1: Conceptual Definitions (Bursik and Grasmick, 1993)

Neighborhood	The smallest geographic area with a name known both to its residents and outsiders
Socioeconomic Composition	The economic structure of a neighborhood.
Residential Stability	The amount of change in population in a neighborhood.
Racial/Ethnic Heterogeneity	Diversity in racial and ethnic composition of a neighborhood.
Primary Relationships	Density of family and friendship networks.
Secondary Relationships	Density of neighborhood
Public Control	The ability of a neighborhood to obtain public goods and services.
Parochial Control	The ability of a neighborhood to supervise and control its own members as well as outsiders who may come into the neighborhood.
Disorder	Violation of norms concerning public behavior (loitering teens, graffiti, vacant buildings, public intoxication, garbage on the street, etc.)
Crime Rate	The rate of crime in a particular neighborhood.
Fear of Crime	Judgment of personal safety in the neighborhood.

population make it difficult to establish and maintain intimate primary ties or secondary ties within the community. Of the structural variables theorized to impact neighborhood social control, they believe that residential stability is the most important.

Racial and ethnic heterogeneity refers to the diversity of neighborhoods in terms of racial and ethnic composition. Heterogeneity is expected to impede communication between residents, limiting the breadth of primary and secondary relationships in neighborhoods (Bursik and Grasmick, 1993).

Primary relational networks refers to the density of family and friendship networks. It is expected that when there are many family networks in a neighborhood it is easier to supervise and provide social control over children (Bursik and Grasmick, 1993).

Secondary relationships refers to the degree of neighborhood interaction. Do neighbors frequently visit each other, borrow items, talk, and interact or are they isolated from each other? The quality and density of neighborhood interaction is expected to increase the use of parochial social control (Bursik and Grasmick, 1993).

Parochial control refers to the ability of neighborhoods to supervise their own residents and outsiders to the neighborhood. It refers to the formation of neighborhood watch groups, casual observation of neighborhood streets, questioning of strangers about suspicious activities, or chastening youth for inappropriate behavior (Bursik and Grasmick, 1993).

The public level of control involves the ability of a community to obtain public goods and services (e.g., health services, social services, policing, etc.) from agencies outside the local community. In the area of crime control, the ability to obtain funds and support for neighborhood watch groups and other crime control measures is expected to play an important role in neighborhood crime control, as well as a neighborhood's relationship with the local police department (Bursik and Grasmick, 1993).

Bursik and Grasmick (1993) discuss in length the problems surrounding the definition of disorder. They seem to rely on a definition provided by Skogan (1990). Disorder is a violation of norms concerning public behavior. Skogan breaks this definition down further into social and physical disorder. Social disorder refers to acts such as public drinking, the presence of loitering youth, panhandling, visible drug use, and harassment. Physical disorder refers to abandoned buildings, the presence of graffiti, visible trash, and unmaintained homes and lawns.

Bursik and Grasmick (1993) provide a review of the use of crime as a dependent variable in the criminological literature. They believe that in definitions of crime the perception of threat is what is important. Thus, they make it clear that their theory applies primarily to those crimes for which widespread consensus exists, and refer to the index crimes from the Uniform Crime Reports as an appropriate measure of crime.

Bursik and Grasmick (1993) discuss the different definitions and operationalization of the concept fear of crime. For example, this concept has been measured in terms of perceived risk, concern, worry, and anxiety. Thus, contradictory findings in this area may be explained by how fear has been conceptualized in the past.

They do not provide a clear definition of fear of crime other than to say that it reflects an emotional response to neighborhood stimuli. Bursik and Grasmick state that "how afraid are you to walk alone at night" has emerged as a standard indicator of fear of crime. This is the type of measure used in this study and the only measures of fear of crime available from the "Crime Changes in Baltimore data.

However, Bursik and Grasmick note that the nature of the perceived victimization is unclear in such items. They also refer to the research of Warr and Stafford (1983) who have provided strong evidence that fear of crime can only be understood fully within an offense-specific framework. Therefore, it is important to note the conceptual and measurement differences in fear of crime research and admit that the measures used in this study may not fully capture this concept. A discussion of measurement issues concerning fear of crime is provided later in this book.

Before introducing the methodology of this research, it is important to review previous ecological literature related to Bursik and Grasmick's theory.

CHAPTER 3

Previous Ecological Research

INTRODUCTION

After a sharp decline in ecological studies in the 1960s, the past two decades have witnessed an increase in research focused on variations in crime rates between communities (Byrne & Sampson, 1986; Bursik, 1988). Similar to the ecological studies conducted by Shaw and McKay, the general thesis of this research has been that characteristics of ecological units have social effects on crime that are not solely attributable to the characteristics of individuals.

However, recent research has departed from the Shaw and McKay studies in several important respects. First, the vast majority of recent research has been conducted not at the local community level but at much higher levels of aggregation such as the city, county, or standard metropolitan statistical area (SMSA) (Sampson, 1990). Also, the variables used in recent studies have expanded beyond economic status, racial composition, and mobility to include factors such as inequality, density, housing structure, social setting, family disruption, and opportunities for crime (Sampson and Lauritsen, 1994).

The first section of this literature review examines Shaw and McKay's Social Disorganization theory in some detail. Second, the literature pertaining to the central concepts in Bursik and Grasmick's theory is reviewed in the following section along with conceptual and measurement problems with previous ecological research.

SHAW AND MCKAY'S SOCIAL DISORGANIZATION THEORY

Introduction

In an introduction to the first edition of *Juvenile Delinquency in Urban Areas*, Ernest Burgess (1942) referred to the work of Shaw and McKay as a "magnum opus in criminology (p. ix)." Their research is essentially the first and most detailed longitudinal study of the life of a city as it relates to crime and delinquency. Although their work is now over a half century old, as Short (1972) points out, "the foundation laid by Shaw and McKay not only has stood the test of time but remains of vital significance for contemporary research and theory." (p. xlii).

Previous Ecological Studies

Many criminology textbooks are written as though Shaw and McKay's ecological research concerning crime and delinquency had no predecessors. They recognized previous ecological research in the first chapter of *Juvenile Delinquency and Urban Areas*. For instance, André Guerry in 1833 computed crime rates, based on number of people accused of crime during the period 1825-30, in eighty-three departments in France (Vold, Bernard, and Snipes, 1998). His studies demonstrated a wide variation in crimes against persons and property.

Henry Mayhew (1862) conducted a large ecological study of crime and delinquency in 41 counties of England and Whales. This study included a series of maps showing the incidence of several types of crime by county. In some counties, the rate of crime was four times that of other counties. In discussing "low neighborhoods" Mayhew states:

> "There are thousands of neglected children loitering about the low neighborhoods of the metropolis, and prowling about the streets, begging and stealing for their daily bread. ... Some are orphans and have no one to care for them; others have left their homes and live in lodging-houses in the most improvident manner, never thinking of tomorrow; others are sent out by their unprincipled parents to beg and steal for a livelihood; others are the children of poor but honest and industrious people, who have been led to steal through the bad companionship of juvenile thieves, ... they have been surrounded by the most baneful and degrading influences..." (p. 273).

In 1856 John Glyde published a study demonstrating large differences in crime and delinquency rates between different cities in the same county and between urban and rural areas (Glyde, 1856). Glyde appeared to conclude that there were tremendous differences in the "moral tendencies" of inhabitants by district, town, and villages within Suffolk County, England.

Cesare Lombroso and other Italian criminologists are widely cited (and often lampooned) for their biological theories of crime causation, but they also examined the ecological distribution of crime in Italy. Discussing the incidence of crime in various areas of Italy, Lombroso (1911) makes the following statement:

> "In every part of Italy, almost in every province, there exists some village renowned for having furnished an unbroken series of special delinquents. Thus, in Liguria, Lerice is proverbial for swindlers, Camofreddo and Mason for homicides, Pozzolo for highway robberies. In the province of

Lucca, Capannori is noted for its assassinations, and Carde in Piedmont for its field thefts. In southern Italy, Soro, Melfi, and St. Fele have always had their bandits since 1860, and the same is true of Partinico and Monreale in Sicily" (pp. 23-24).

Shaw and McKay were not the first to conduct ecological studies on crime and delinquency in America or for that matter, in Chicago. Breckinridge and Abbott in 1912 published a document illustrating the distribution of crime and delinquency in Chicago. They mapped the homes of boys and girls brought before the Juvenile Court of Cook County on petitions alleging delinquency between 1899 and 1909. In a precursor to Shaw and McKay they make the following statement:

"A study of this neighborhood makes possible several conclusions with regard to "delinquent neighborhoods." It becomes clear, in the first place, that the region from which the children of the court chiefly comes is the densely populated West Side, and that the most conspicuous centers of delinquency in this section have been the congested wards which lie among the river and the canals...." (p. 150-51).

As Shaw and McKay (1972) point out, this study did not compute the rates of crime and delinquency for the various neighborhoods of Chicago. Thus, the concentration of cases by city region could have been due to the density of the population.

Other studies in America were conducted by Ernest Burgess in Kansas and R.D. McKenzie in Columbus, Ohio. All came to the general conclusion that delinquency and crime rates varied widely from neighborhood to neighborhood. The point of this review is to demonstrate that Shaw and McKay had a number of ecological studies to draw from in the development of their own research, and that these authors are not due all credit for the origins of an ecological approach to crime and delinquency.

Methodology of the Chicago Area Studies

Shaw and McKay utilized two distinct methodological approaches in their studies of urban areas. First of all they obtained several forms of official agency data including census reports, juvenile court data, and housing and welfare records. From census, housing and welfare records they were able to develop measures of substandard housing, population change, economic and racial segregation, "families on relief" (welfare dependence), distribution of immigrant populations, infant mortality, tuberculosis, and mental disease. From juvenile court records they developed measures of the distribution of youth arrested and brought before the court, committed to correctional schools, and youth contacts with police probation officers.

These measures were applied to the city of Chicago in graphic form as well as displayed in charts and tables. The data was gathered over a twenty year period and demonstrated tremendous consistency in neighborhood problems despite a complete shift in the population of people who occupied those areas.

The second method of study employed by Shaw and McKay was the life history or case study approach. They wrote detailed life histories of Chicago youth documenting the development of their delinquent careers. From this work came three classic portraits of delinquent street life; *The Jackroller* (1930), *The Natural History of a Delinquent Career* (1931) and *Brothers in Crime* (1938). It is from the case study approach that Shaw and McKay developed their theoretical insights into the processes involved in becoming delinquent in inner-city neighborhoods.

Findings and Theoretical Propositions

There were a number of important findings documented in *Juvenile Delinquency and Urban Areas*. From official agency data, Shaw and McKay (1972) observed several important correlations concerning Chicago neighborhoods (they were well aware that the relationships they found did not establish a causal relationship). Listed below are some of the more salient points:

- High delinquency neighborhoods were found within or near areas of heavy industry. These areas also had the highest number of condemned buildings and the greatest evidence of physical disorder.

- The population of high delinquency neighborhoods was decreasing. Shaw and McKay suggested that the rapid population change was due to industrial invasion of these neighborhoods resulting in fewer residential areas.

- The highest rates of delinquency, as well as other social ills such as infant deaths, tuberculosis, and mental illness, were found in low socioeconomic areas (measured by welfare dependence, median rentals, and percentage of home-ownership). Importantly, Shaw and McKay did not believe there was a direct causal relationship between socioeconomic status and delinquency; observing that delinquency rates remained stable for the city as a whole during the Great Depression.

- High delinquency neighborhoods were associated with immigrant and African-American populations. In order to examine whether delinquency was associated with "particular types of people", as was the popular explanation at the time, they further analyzed their data and found that many urban neighborhoods retained their high delinquency rates despite almost entire shifts of the population in these areas. For example, approximately ninety percent of the population in eight urban neighborhoods in 1884 was composed of German, Irish, English, Scottish, or Scandinavian ethnic groups. By 1930, approximately eighty-five percent of these neighborhoods were composed of Czech, Polish, Slavic, or other ethnic groups. These neighborhoods had the highest delinquency rates of the city despite the dramatic shift in ethnic populations. Additionally, no ethnic or racial group exhibited a uniform delinquency rate in all parts of the city. The overall delinquency rate of a particular group was associated with the frequency of members of that group in high delinquency neighborhoods.

It is difficult to emphasize enough the importance of these findings to the field of criminology, especially the last finding. It signified a change from psychological and biological explanations of crime and delinquency to a sociological approach. An examination of the membership of the American Society of Criminology or coverage of criminology as a discipline in textbooks is an indicator of how much the field is dominated by sociologists. That dominance began with the Chicago School sociologists.

As Shaw and McKay clearly understood, correlations of neighborhood characteristics with delinquency rates and other social problems do not provide an explanation for the *causes* of delinquency. Nor did these researchers believe that rapid population change or socioeconomic status was directly related to delinquency. For that explanation they relied primarily on extensive interviews or case histories of delinquent youth and other citizens of delinquent neighborhoods.

The central theoretical argument by Shaw and McKay was that rapid population change in many urban neighborhoods resulted in a breakdown in formal social organizations and traditions. It is within these formal organizations, traditions, and public opinion that a neighborhood normally controls the conduct of its members, especially its youth. Residents in neighborhoods of rapid social change are less likely to know one another and thus are less likely to supervise neighborhood youth. Other observations that Shaw and McKay (1972) made include the following:

"...In areas of low rates of delinquents there is more or less uniformity, consistency, and universality of conventional values and attitudes with respect to child care, conformity to law, and related matters; whereas in the high-rate areas systems of competing and conflicting moral values have developed" (Shaw and McKay, 1972; p. 170).

"Children living in such communities are exposed to a variety of contradictory standards and forms of behavior rather than to a relatively consistent and conventional pattern" (p. 172).

"The heavy concentration of delinquency in certain areas means ... that boys living in these areas are in contact not only with individuals who engage in proscribed activity but also with groups which sanction such behavior and exert pressure upon their members to conform to group standards" (p. 174).

The above statements recognize that there is not a consensus in values either for or against criminality in high delinquency neighborhoods and that there is a constant battle among neighborhood residents concerning conflicting beliefs over appropriate behavior. These statements are also important precursors to cultural and subcultural theories of delinquency as well as to Sutherland's Differential Association theory.

Another observation by Shaw and McKay was that delinquent neighborhoods provided tremendous opportunities for immersion in a delinquent career that included fencing stolen goods, auto theft, jackrolling, and the rackets. Conventional opportunities in these neighborhoods were lacking. This observation no doubt influenced Cloward and Ohlin's Differential Opportunity theory.

Shaw and McKay's examination of juvenile court records and their interviews with delinquent youth pointed to the overwhelming group nature of delinquency. The concentration of delinquents in certain neighborhoods exacerbated the impact of delinquent peers and is an indication that delinquent values are transmitted from generation to generation.

In an important statement that predates Merton's Anomie theory concerning societal social order, Shaw and McKay summarize:

"it is assumed that the differentiation of areas and the segregation of population within the city have resulted in wide variation of opportunities in the struggle for position within our social order. The groups in the areas of lowest economic status find themselves at a disadvantage in the struggle to achieve the goals idealized in civilization. These differences are translated into conduct through the general struggle for those economic symbols, which signify a desirable position in the larger social order. Those persons who occupy a disadvantageous position are involved in a conflict between the goals assumed to be attainable in a free society and those actually attainable for a large proportion of the population" (pp. 186-7).

Finally, in a statement that predates labeling theorists by several decades, Shaw and McKay claimed that once a delinquent career is established, a delinquent youth begins

"to identify himself with the criminal world, and to embody in his own philosophy of life the moral values which prevailed in the criminal groups which he had contact" (Shaw, 1931; p. 233).

They also documented that delinquent youth often felt rejected and stigmatized by their community.

The observations noted above make it clear that Shaw and McKay developed a large number of theoretical insights by their studies of Chicago neighborhoods. It is also clear that many of these observations had a large influence on the future of criminology as a field. They influenced directly or indirectly almost every traditional sociological theory to follow.

Criticisms of Social Disorganization Theory

There are a large number of criticisms of Shaw and McKay's Social Disorganization theory (for a complete review see Bursik, 1988). Kornhauser (1978) notes that Shaw and McKay did not make clear the causal connections between social disorganization and neighborhood delinquency rates. Kornhauser claims that Shaw and McKay draw freely on elements of strain, cultural conflict, and control theories, but the implications of those theories are at times inconsistent. Kornhauser was particularly concerned with the integration of cultural and control theory arguments. Sampson (1997) has argued that these types of arguments are not necessarily incongruent.

Additionally, I would argue that the work of Shaw and McKay was of an inductive nature. They systematically made observations of Chicago neighborhoods over a period of time and teased out the implications of their observations into theoretical statements. They did not use their data to test a theory. They used their data to begin the development of theoretical ideas. As previously stated these ideas had an enormous impact on the field. In no section or chapter of *Juvenile Delinquency and Urban Areas* do Shaw and McKay attempt to make a formal statement of a theory. Thus, their work should not be evaluated in such a manner.

Other arguments concerning measuring the concept of social disorganization and tests of the theory have been only recently clarified. Because of a lack of a clear definition of social disorganization, some (Lander, 1954; Pfohl, 1985) confused this concept with the phenomenon it was intended to explain (delinquency rates). Recent theoretical elaborations by Sampson and others have cleared this conceptual confusion.

More importantly, early and even some recent tests of the theory had not gone beyond the work of Shaw and McKay themselves. These studies either relied on correlations between ecological characteristics of neighborhoods and crime or delinquency or they relied on very crude measures of social disorganization (Bursik, 1988). The reason for this is due to the difficulty of developing social process measures of social disorganization such as ability to supervise youth, organizational participation, and other important indicators of social disorganization.

Those type of measures require interviews or surveys. Additionally, multiple regression and multi-level statistical techniques have not been widely used until recent years. It is for these reasons that Sampson and Groves argued that Social Disorganization theory had never been tested until they conducted such a test in 1989.

SOCIOECONOMIC COMPOSITION

Not surprisingly, most recent neighborhood-based studies of crime and delinquency have emphasized dimensions of social status and economic inequality. Unlike Shaw and McKay, however, the majority of these studies have employed multivariate methods that seek to estimate the effects of economic structure independent of other factors.

Recent studies utilizing victimization rates have questioned the strength of the effects of poverty and income inequality on crime once other factors are controlled. Sampson (1986a) utilized Bureau of the Census neighborhood characteristics data in conjunction with victimization data from the National Crime Survey. Results derived from analysis of variance indicated that poverty and inequality exhibited weak or insignificant effects on violent victimization compared to density of housing, residential mobility, and family structure. The effect of income inequality on violent victimization disappeared once racial composition and divorce rates were controlled.

Smith and Jarjoura (1988) found a similar pattern in another victimization study. In this study interviews were conducted with approximately 200 people in 57 neighborhoods in Rochester, New York, Tampa-St. Petersburg, Florida, and St. Louis, Missouri. In a test of Shaw and McKay's social disorganization model, they found a significant interaction between mobility and low-income in explaining violence. Specifically, mobility was positively associated with violent crime rates in poorer neighborhoods but not in more affluent areas. The main effects of mobility and income were not significant when the interaction term was in the model. The authors concluded that communities characterized by high levels of poverty and rapid population turnover have significantly higher crime rates than either mobile areas that are more affluent or poor areas that are more stable.

RESIDENTIAL STABILITY

A central argument of Shaw and McKay (1942) was that population change undermined the social control mechanisms of a community. Specifically, a high rate of mobility, especially in areas of decreasing population, was expected to encourage institutional disruption and weaken community controls. There has been a good deal of empirical support for this proposition.

For example, Block's (1979) study in Chicago revealed negative correlations between percent neighborhood stability and the violent crimes of homicide, robbery, and aggravated assault. As already mentioned, Smith and Jarjoura (1988) found a significant positive effect of neighborhood mobility (percentage of households occupied by persons who lived there less than three years) on rates of violence only in low-income neighborhoods. This interaction of mobility and poverty was the largest factor in explaining violence in their study.

Victimization data form the National Crime Survey indicated that residential mobility has significant positive effects on rates of violent victimization (Sampson, 1985). After controlling for other neighborhood-level correlates of victimization, violent victimization rates for residents of high-mobility neighborhoods were twice those of residents in low-mobility areas (Sampson, 1985; 1986a).

Although mobility rates of an area have consistently been associated with delinquency in cross-sectional designs, until recently, few studies have actually considered processes of neighborhood change in a longitudinal design (Exceptions include Bursik and Webb, 1982; Heitgard and Bursik, 1987). Taylor and Covington (1988) examined changes in community structure and homicide and aggravated assault in 277 Baltimore neighborhoods. They found that the increasing entrenchment of the urban underclass in the form of increasing poverty and minority concentration was linked to increases in violence. Also, gentrifying neighborhoods that were experiencing rapid change in terms of unexpected increases in owner-occupied housing, one-unit structures, and changes in family status also experienced large increases in violence.

Existing research suggests that there is a consistent relationship between rates of mobility and delinquency. Furthermore, this relationship appears especially salient when linked to community change in general, and especially in the form of increased poverty in ghetto neighborhoods (Schuerman and Kobrin, 1986; Rose and McCain, 1990).

RACIAL AND ETHNIC HETEROGENEITY

While racial and ethnic heterogeneity played an important role in Shaw and McKay's research, in their writings they generally referred to population composition. The reason for this is that their data indicated that delinquency rates were higher in predominately African American/foreign-born areas than in areas of maximum heterogeneity.

In similar fashion, most research on delinquency has examined racial composition (usually percent African American) rather than racial heterogeneity. Research consistently indicates that percent African American is positively and strongly related to rates of delinquency. For example, Block (1979) demonstrated that violence rates were significantly and substantially related to percent African American. Other studies showed similar findings (Beasley and Antunes, 1974; Mladenka and Hill (1976); Messner and Tardiff, 1986; Sampson, 1985; Roncek et al., 1981; and Smith and Jarjoura, 1988).

The dispute is over the strength of the direct effect of racial composition on violence. Some researchers report that the effect of percent African American on delinquency remains strong even after controlling for other factors (e.g., Beasley and Antunes, 1974; Roncek et al., 1981), while others claim that the effect of race sharply attenuates once other factors are controlled (e.g., Block, 1979; Curry and Spergal, 1988; Messner and Tardiff, 1986).

One of the few exceptions to composition measures was a probability-based measure of racial heterogeneity developed by Smith and Jarjoura (1988). This measure was developed by calculating the probability that two randomly selected individuals from a neighborhood will be members of different racial groups. This measure of heterogeneity was significantly related to delinquency independent of mobility and poverty. However, the effect of heterogeneity was rendered insignificant once family structure (percent single-parent families) was controlled.

Thus, the research evidence clearly indicates that percent African American and heterogeneity are strong correlates of delinquency. However, it is less clear whether racial composition or heterogeneity has unique explanatory power.

DISORDER

Few researchers have devoted as much time and energy on the consequences of physical disorder on community stability and urban decline than Wesley Skogan. Skogan

(1990) combined survey data from 40 residential neighborhoods in Chicago, Philadelphia, San Francisco, Atlanta, Houston, and Newark, New Jersey between 1977 and 1983. Roughly 13,000 adults were asked about their victimization experiences, the extent of various forms of disorder in their immediate area, and their satisfaction with the neighborhood. Additionally, within ten of the 40 neighborhoods, field researchers conducted extensive observations and interviews concerning how individuals and organizations react to crime problems resulting in 10,000 pages of field notes.

Skogan (1990) recognizes that the term disorder is somewhat ambiguous and our conceptions of the concept are subject to change over time. However, the dimensions of disorder he describes appear to be widely agreed upon regardless of class, race, or age. Skogan describes disorder in terms of its social and physical dimensions. Survey respondents ranked public drinking highest among social disorders, followed by loitering youth (corner gangs), and reports of drug use. Problems with noisy neighbors, panhandling, and harassment were rated less highly. Concern about street prostitution and sexually oriented businesses ranked among the highest concerns, but only in those few neighborhoods where it was concentrated.

While Skogan discusses the problems in defining disorder, he does not discuss the tautological problem of utilizing measures of disorder such as vandalism, public drinking, and fighting and arguing, which are also in many jurisdictions defined as criminal behavior. Skogan (1990) admits that the only real difference between crime and many disorders is that either politicians have not enacted some widely agreed upon values into law, or the police do not generally enforce disorderly behavior that is also illegal.

Skogan (1990) states that the distinction between disorder and crime is that the former presents visual cues to neighborhood residents that signal a breakdown of the local social order. The importance of disorder is the reaction to it by citizens in the community. In this way, disorder is viewed as an independent variable having a causal impact on neighborhood social control.

The other important distinction is that disorderly behavior, when and where it is also illegal behavior, is considered more of a public nuisance than a crime. In fact, these behaviors are rarely enforced by law enforcement, whereas the index crimes (murder, aggravated assault, robbery, rape, burglary, and felony theft) are frequently enforced (Skogan, 1990).

Physical disorders are more enduring aspects of a neighborhood's physical environment. Skogan (1990) found that there was considerable variation in the extent of urban decay. Vandalism was the most highly ranked problem in all study sites, followed by litter and trash, garbage handling, junk strewn vacant lots, and dog litter. Building abandonment and trash-filled vacant lots were low on the list of problems overall, but ranked high in a few neighborhoods where this type of disorder persisted.

It is suggested by Wilson and Kelling (1982) that one of the consequences of disorder are more serious crime problems. Resident's sense of territoriality shrinks, untended property becomes fair game to plunder, and tolerance for disorder invites outside offenders. To test this hypothesis, Skogan (1990) compared levels of disorder to reports of robbery victimization. After controlling for poverty, stability, and neighborhood composition, high disorder neighborhoods were strongly related to reports of robbery. Additionally, Skogan's (1990) research clearly suggests that disorder is negatively related to neighborhood interpersonal relationships measured by mutual helping behavior.

Disorder and Community Reactions

There are competing views about the relationship between people's concern about a problem and their willingness to take action.   The two could be related positively, negatively, or in a curvilinear fashion, and this relationship may differ from one form of action to another.   The positive view is that concern stimulates action.   Emile Durkheim argued that crime has an integrative function. I t shocks the sentiments of ordinary people by threatening their lives, families, property, and their views of appropriate behavior.   This affront to their values leads them to act individually and more importantly, collectively to do something in response.

One observer in Skogan's (1990) studies when questioned about block organizations in his neighborhood stated:

> "the 16th street area is organized to control porno shops in the area, with the eventual goal of eliminating them entirely. Their second goal is to bring new money into the area by influencing banks to provide low interest loans to interested homeowners and small business people... Their success in keeping porno shops out are numerous. The Roxi theater, which was one of the more sleazy porno theaters in San Francisco had its lease revoked by the owners and is now run by progressive members of the community. Landlords of existing porno bookstores have agreed not to renew the leases of the stores in their buildings" (p. 67).

During the 1970s, the belief underlying several federal crime prevention programs was that people living in high-crime   neighborhoods   would,   with   only   a   little encouragement, form neighborhood organizations for their own protection (Lewis, 1979).

The negative view is that concern actually discourages constructive responses to problems. There has been little research on the consequences of disorder, but fear of crime does not appear to stimulate positive responses to crime (Tyler, 1984). In fact, surveys and experiments generally indicate that high levels of fear reduce people's willingness to take positive action when they see crimes being committed- many balk even at simply calling the police. Past research suggests several reasons why disorder might undermine a community's capacity to act collectively.

First, perceptions registered in surveys that "neighbors help each other" appear to be an important indicator of morale in urban communities, and are related to a variety of positive actions against crime. Without such support, people feel powerless, impotent, and vulnerable in the face of crime. In past studies, high levels of disorder appear to undermine the belief that problems can be solved locally; they increase people's sense of personal isolation, and spread the perception that no one will come to their rescue when they find themselves in trouble (Lewis and Salem, 1986).

Second, perceptions of disorder, like fear of crime, may shrink the circumference of the turf that individuals feel responsible for defending. When the boundaries of their watchfulness are wide, neighborhood residents monitor the behavior of more youths, keep an eye on more strangers, and investigate more suspicious sounds and activities (Skogan, 1990).

Where territories encompass only people's own homes and families, untended persons and property are fair game for plunder. Territoriality is an important component of the larger process of surveillance, which may be an important mechanism for controlling crime. Surveillance entails both watching and acting. Acting is facilitated by personal recognition; hence the importance of knowing your neighbors. It is also facilitated by the sense that local standards about appropriate public behavior are widely shared; this legitimizes individual intervention (Skogan, 1990). There is some evidence (Shotland and Goldstein, 1984) that crime is encouraged by low levels of surveillance of public places, and reduced by people's willingness to challenge strangers, supervise youths, and step forward as witnesses.

However, in neighborhoods in decline, mutual distrust and hostility are more common, and antipathy between newcomers and long-term residents prevails. Residents of poor, heterogeneous areas tend to view each other with suspicion (Taub, Taylor, and Dunham, 1984; Greenberg et al., 1982). Sarah Boggs found that African American central-city residents were less likely than other Missourians to think their neighbors would take responsibility for neighborhood safety, and less likely to think their neighbors would call the police if they saw a crime.

Skogan's (1990) study on the impacts of disorder found just this negative relationship. He tested this question by asking respondents if they would characterize their neighborhoods as places "where people help one another" or "people go their own way." He found support for the negative view. Controlling for poverty, stability, and racial composition, where levels of disorder were high, respondents reported that people go their own way. Nearly the same results occurred when respondents were asked whether they had a neighbor watch their home when they went away. In neighborhoods marked by disorder, fewer people were willing to ask their neighbors to watch their homes and fewer stated they had plans to remain in the neighborhood.

A somewhat more complex non-linear hypothesis is that excessive levels of disorder are debilitating, but moderate levels of disorder are constructive. Those who think their area is virtually problem-free would have few reasons to engage in problem-solving activities, while at the high end of the scale demoralization and distrust may prevail; in this view, community capacity would be highest in places facing middling disorder, where there are visible problems but they are not overwhelming.

There is a great deal of interest in neighborhood watch programs in Britain, and a national survey there found just this pattern: middle-range levels of concern- were most strongly related to support for neighborhood watch (Hope and Hough, 1988). This suggests that the effects of disorder are curvilinear. Neighborhoods with very high levels of disorder and very low levels of disorder would be expected to be the least likely to organize to combat their problems.

PRIMARY AND SECONDARY RELATIONSHIPS

The structural dimensions of community social organization have been measured in terms of the prevalence and interdependence of informal (e.g., density of friendship ties and acquaintanceship) and formal social networks (e.g., organizational participation) in a community and in the extent of collective supervision that the community directs to local problems.

This approach is grounded in what Sampson (1988) calls the systemic model. The local community is seen as a complex system of friendship and kinship networks, and formal and informal associational ties rooted in family life. The systemic model has also been defined as social organization or social disorganization. Social organization and social disorganization are at opposite ends of a spectrum with respect to systemic networks of community social control. Bursik (1988) suggests that when social disorganization is defined in this manner, it is clearly separable not only from the processes that may lead to it (e.g., poverty, mobility, ethnic heterogeneity), but also from the level of criminal behavior that may be a result.[6]

When residents form local social ties, their capacity for community control increases because they are better able to recognize strangers and are more apt to engage in guardianship behavior against victimization (Taylor et al., 1984; Skogan, 1986). Also, the greater the density of friendship networks among those in a community, the greater is the constraint on delinquency within the purview of the social network (Krohn, 1986).

Another dimension of secondary relationships concerns the rate of local participation in formal and voluntary organizations. Community organizations reflect the structural essence of local community solidarity (Hunter, 1974). Kornhauser (1978) states that institutional instability and the isolation of community institutions are important conditions underlying the structural dimension of social disorganization. Her argument is that when links between community institutions are weak the capacity of a community to defend its local interests is weakened. Shaw and McKay (1969), and more recently Taylor et al. (1984) and Simcha-Fagan and Schwartz (1986) have also argued that a weak community organizational base serves to attenuate local social control functions regarding youth.

There has been renewed interest lately in testing the structural dimensions of social disorganization. Taylor et al. (1984) examined variations in violent crime across 63 street blocks in Baltimore in 1978. The authors constructed block-level measures of what they termed social ties and near-home responsibilities. The former measured the proportion of respondents who belonged to an organization to which co-residents also belonged. The latter measured

---

[6] One of the criticisms of Shaw and McKay's theory was that the concept of social disorganization was indistinguishable from what it was attempting to explain.

tapped the extent to which respondents felt responsible for what happened in the area surrounding their home.

Both of these dimensions of informal social control were significantly related to community-level variations in violence. Taylor et al. (1984) also showed that blocks with higher neighborhood identification, as indicated by the proportion of residents who were able to provide a neighborhood name, had significantly lower rates of violence.

Simcha-Fagan and Schwartz (1986) examined survey data from 553 residents of 12 different neighborhoods in New York City. They found a significant negative relationship between the rate of self-reported delinquency and rates of organizational participation. The authors concluded that level of organizational participation had a significant positive effect on school attachment, which had a negative effect on self-reported delinquency. The level of organizational participation also had a small direct effect on self-reported delinquency.

Sampson and Groves (1989) utilized the British Crime Survey (BCS), a nationwide survey of England and Wales, to examine dimensions of social disorganization. The sample was drawn from more than 200 ecological areas that was representative of a relatively small, homogenous locality that approximated the concept of local community. The authors reported that the presence of unsupervised peer groups in a community had the largest overall effect on rates of victimization in Great Britain. Also, local friendship networks had a significant and substantial negative effect on robbery, whereas rates of organizational participation had significant inverse effects on robbery and stranger violence.

Finally, Elliott et al. (1996) recently examined survey data collected in 1990 from neighborhoods in Chicago and Denver. The Denver site is based on data from over 1,500 youth living in over 30 block groups. The Chicago site is based on data collected from approximately 500 African American, predominantly poor families residing in more than 50 Chicago census tracts. The authors found that the effects of neighborhood disadvantage on adolescent problem behavior and prosocial competence, were largely mediated by a measure of informal social control at both sites. The higher the level of informal control, conceptualized as the number of neighbors willing to intervene when various unlawful acts occurred in respondents' neighborhoods, the lower the levels of adolescent problem behavior.

These empirical results suggest that communities characterized by sparse friendship networks, and low organizational participation had disproportionately high rates of delinquency. Importantly, variations in the structural dimensions largely mediated the effects of community social status, residential mobility, and ethnic heterogeneity.

Social Disorganization and the Public Level of Direct Control

Bursik and Grasmick (1993) suggest that the greatest shortcoming of the basic social disorganization model is the failure to consider the public sphere of social control. By the public sphere they refer to the "ability of a community to obtain goods and services that are allocated by agencies located outside the neighborhood" (p. 17).

The external resources to which Bursik and Grasmick (1993) refer are of two types. First, neighborhoods may attempt to organize to confront crime problems. They argue the success of these organizations depends on their ability to influence municipal bureaucracies and public/private decision-making agencies to deliver needed economic resources.

The relationship between the neighborhood and the local police department is the second external resource concerning the control of crime (Bursik and Grasmick, 1993). They point to research that suggests that offenders choose targets based on differential patterns of law enforcement (Carter and Hill, 1978; Rengert and Walsilchick, 1985). They also point out that there is inconsistent evidence concerning the influence of neighborhood characteristics on the delivery of police services (Smith, 1986; Slovak, 1987).

Bursik and Grasmick (1993) argue that traditional social disorganization studies have narrowly focused on resident interpersonal networks in communities to the exclusion of networks to the public sphere of control. They suggest that this may be the reason several studies find stable neighborhoods with extensive interpersonal networks that have relatively high rates of crime and delinquency (Whyte, 1981; Suttles, 1968; Moore, 1978; Horowitz, 1983).

Lewis and Salem (1986) argue that it is very difficult to significantly affect neighborhood life through the efforts of local community organizations alone. Rather, these groups must be able to effectively negotiate with those agencies that make decisions regarding the investment of resources to communities. Whyte (1981: 273) argues that the problems he witnessed in the Cornerville section of Boston were largely due to the lack of effective ties between the neighborhood and the broader society. Suttles (1968) makes a similar argument.

Dawley's (1992) account of the Vice Lord's in Chicago illustrates the possible importance of external resources. Between 1968 and 1969 the Vice Lords were able to solicit funds from the Rockefeller and Ford Foundations to develop a series of neighborhood-based programs. Dawley (1992) states that gang activity and fear of crime decreased during this time. However, funding for the programs ended after a dispute with the city over taxes. Most of the lords either reentered gangs or were dead within ten years.

FEAR OF CRIME

Over the last 25 years fear of crime has emerged as an important research topic (McGarrell et al., 1997). The topic has been considered important because fear of crime does not necessarily correlate with actual victimization. For example, women and the elderly are among the most fearful of crime yet are among the lowest demographic groups in actual victimization. Young men do not report high levels of fear of crime and yet are the most likely to be a victim of violent crime. From this research four distinct theoretical models have developed to explain fear of crime. The models and related empirical research are reviewed below. How each model relates to Bursik and Grasmick's theory is discussed.

The Indirect Victimization Model

The earliest research on fear of crime was based on a victimization model. This model theorized that fear of crime was directly related to being a victim of crime. Although Skogan and Maxfield (1981) found a relationship between victimization and fear, others found that victimization was either unrelated or only minimally related to fear (Gates and Rohe, 1987; Liska, Sanchirico, and Reed, 1988). This model was also questioned because of the consistent finding that those most likely to be victims (young males) had relatively low levels of fear, whereas those least likely to be victims of crime (elderly females) had relatively high levels of fear (Garofalo and Laub, 1978). These findings led to the development of an indirect victimization model.

The indirect victimization model is based on the idea that groups who perceive themselves vulnerable to crime will have higher levels of fear. Thus the finding that women are least likely to be victimized yet have high levels of fear is attributed to women's perceptions of greater physical vulnerability to offenders. Similarly, the finding that lower socioeconomic groups and African Americans have higher fear levels is interpreted as a consequence of heightened social vulnerability (Skogan and Maxfield, 1981). This model also predicts higher rates of fear for those embedded in social networks. A high level of social interaction is believed to lead to the learning of victimization of others in the neighborhood (Lewis and Salem, 1986).

The indirect victimization model suggests that neighborhood socioeconomic status may have a direct effect on fear of crime. High levels of friendship and familial networks, as defined by Bursik and Grasmick, may serve to heighten fear in a neighborhood. This model also suggests the need to control for demographic variables such as age, sex, gender, and previous victimization when attempting to explain fear of crime.

The Community Concern Model

The community concern model developed by Taylor and Hale (1986) is closely related to the disorder model. This perspective predicts that fear of crime increases as concerns about the neighborhood increase. Taylor and Hale (1986) found that fear of crime was higher among people who reported their neighborhood as less satisfying. Lewis and Salem (1986) attribute this community concern to the erosion of commonly accepted standards and values. They maintain that fear is a result of the loss of neighborhood social control. Similarly, Taylor et al. (1984)

found that social ties were negatively related to fear of crime. Stranger recognition and community attachment measured as residents who could distinguish strangers from neighbors and who claimed to feel part of the neighborhood reported less fear (Hunter and Baumer, 1982).

The community concern model makes predictions that are very similar to those of Bursik and Grasmick. The empirical research related to the community concern model suggests that residents who are not attached or satisfied with their neighborhood and where there are few social and familial ties in the neighborhood are more likely to have higher levels of fear of crime. Additionally, greater neighborhood social control mediates or inhibits fear of crime.

The Disorder Model

There are a number of variations to the disorder perspective (See Greene and Taylor, 1988, for a discussion of the different forms of the model). The principle argument is that residents in neighborhoods who perceive more signs of disorder in their immediate environment feel more vulnerable and thus more fearful. Signs of disorder or incivilities may be either social, such as public drinking, drug use, fighting and arguing; or physical, such as litter, graffiti, abandoned lots, and vacant housing. These incivilities are theorized as a warning to residents that they are at risk of victimization.

Skogan (1990) observed that disorderly persons are perceived as unpredictable and potentially violent. They may use graffiti and harassment as means of displaying their presence and power. Incivilities may also suggest that widely held norms and values no longer can be counted on to protect neighborhood residents.

The disorder model has received empirical support. Several researchers have found a relationship between fear of crime and perceived social and physical disorder (Gates and Rohe, 1987; LaGrange, Ferraro, and Supancic, 1992; Lewis and Salem, 1986; Skogan and Maxfield, 1981). In a national sample of residents in Great Britain, Hope and Hough (1988) found that the association between disorder and fear was strong even when other aspects of community life were controlled.

In contrast, Taylor et al. (1985) found the relationship between disorder and fear to be conditional. This relationship remained strong in moderate-income neighborhoods but not in the full sample of neighborhoods, once controls for social class were introduced. Additionally, Taylor and Schumaker (1990) found that the effect of neighborhood disorder on fear of crime weakened over time when deterioration reached high levels.

Subcultural Diversity Model

The subcultural diversity model states that fear of crime is a result of living close to others whose cultural background is different from one's own. The more one is surrounded by ethnic subcultural groups whose public behavior is different or foreign, the greater the concern for one's safety. This model suggests that behavior and mannerisms of people belonging to different groups are difficult to interpret and may promote fear (Covington and Taylor, 1991; Merry 1981). A number of researchers have found a relationship between the level of ethnic diversity in an area and fear of crime (Moeller, 1989; Ortega and Myles, 1987; Parker and Ray, 1990).

This perspective is closely associated with Bursik and Grasmick's statements concerning racial/ethnic heterogeneity. Racially diverse neighborhoods are often unstable neighborhoods. This leads to breakdowns in primary and secondary networks and a decreased ability to maintain social control. The development of strong secondary networks is especially problematic because of the distrust that exists between many racial/ethnic groups.

Integrated Models

Bennett and Flavin (1991) developed an integrated model to explain fear of crime using measures of victimization, disorder, and subcultural diversity. They analyzed this model using survey data collected in Newark, New Jersey and Belize City, Belize. They found that the correlates of fear were similar in both settings despite large differences in levels of fear of crime and victimization. Gender, age, social disorder, and subcultural diversity (measured as ethnicity) were the greatest explanatory variables in both models.

A limitation of Bennett and Flavin's study is that it is conducted only at the individual level. Covington and Taylor (1991) argue that the above fear models clearly point to between-neighborhood or ecological processes. Their study combined central concepts from each fear of crime model and distinguished between- and within-neighborhood sources of impact, with data from surveys of 1622 residents of 66 Baltimore neighborhoods and from on-site assessments.

Their results supported the indirect victimization model at both the neighborhood and individual level. Neighborhoods where residents hear of more local burglaries are more fearful as are individuals, who hear of more burglaries, even when disorder in the neighborhood is taken into account. Also, between-neighborhood differences in race and class are associated with higher levels of fear. The disorder model was also supported at both the neighborhood and individual level. The individual level measure of disorder had the strongest relationship to fear of crime[7].

As the community concern model implies, neighborhoods where residents perceive others as less likely to respond to a spray painting incident have higher fear levels. However, within neighborhood differences in such perceptions showed no influence. Finally, Covington and Taylor's analysis supports the subcultural diversity model. Regardless of the respondent's race, those most different racially from their neighbors have more fear.

McGarrell, Giacomazzi, and Thurman (1997) also tested an integrated model from the fear of crime perspectives using individual-level data from Spokane, Washington. They did not test the subcultural diversity model. Their analysis supported the other three perspectives. Importantly, they extended the traditional model by adding inhibitors of fear of crime in the analysis. They found those residential neighborhoods with a large percentage of homeowners, where residents are attached to their neighborhoods, and employ informal means of social control all serve to decrease fear of crime.

Issues In Measuring Fear Of Crime

Haghighi and Sorenson (1996) assert that there are three general methodological problems in measuring fear of crime: interpreting perceived crime risk as fear of crime, emphasizing fear of violent victimization while neglecting the more common nonviolent victimizations, and using ambiguous indicators of crime fear.

---

[7] Importantly, the Baltimore data includes objective neighborhood-level measures of disorder as rated by field researchers as well as an individual-level scale of *perceptions* of disorder. The perception of disorder, not objective measures of disorder, is most closely linked to fear of crime in the Covington and Taylor study.

Ferarro and LaGrange (1987) believe that many researchers have failed to distinguish between risk of victimization and fear of crime. Many opinion researchers ask questions regarding the respondents' crime concern rather than whether they are afraid of becoming victims of crime. Haghighi and Sorenson (1996) assert that the question "How safe would you feel being out alone in your neighborhood at night?," fails to directly measure fear of crime. That type of question reflects a more general safety concern.

Another common problem with fear of crime measures is the overemphasis on fear of personal violent victimization over nonviolent property offenses (Haghighi and Sorensen, 1996). People are much more likely to be the victims of property crimes (Smith and Hill, 1991).

The specificity of fear of crime measures is another concern. Some studies measure fear of crime with a single broad item such as "How fearful are you of being the victim of a serious crime?" LaGrange and Ferraro (1989) argue that this type of question lacks specificity and is prone to error because one cannot determine which crimes one fears. Haghighi and Sorenson (1996) recommend asking respondents how much they worry about particular types of crimes. Warr and Stafford (1983) have also found that fear of crime is a multiplicative function of both the risk of victimization and the seriousness of the potential event.

CONCEPTUAL AND MEASUREMENT PROBLEMS IN ECOLOGICAL RESEARCH

In a detailed review of individual, situational, and macrolevel risk factors in understanding violence, Sampson and Lauritsen (1994) identify several problems in macro level research.

First of all, previous research has frequently inferred the existence of intervening community processes. Several studies reviewed above indicate that factors such as racial heterogeneity, poverty, and educational level predict crime rates, but they often fail to specify the intervening variables between neighborhood structure and crime. Kornhauser (1978) argued that most criminological theories begin with the same independent variables, especially stratification variables such as socioeconomic status. Intervening variables in contextual studies, supplied by competing theories, have not been tested frequently in past research (Sampson and Lauritsen, 1994).

The use of official crime data has also been criticized. The Shaw and McKay research as well as the studies that followed it in the 1950s used officially based crime rates. With respect to community level studies the primary issue with official data concerns ecological biases in official reaction to reports of crime (Hagan et al., 1978; Smith, 1986). In particular, conflict theorists argue that lower-status neighborhoods may have higher delinquency rates in part because police concentration is greater there compared to higher status areas. The type of neighborhood in which police-citizen encounters occur may also influence the actions taken by police (Hagan et al, 1978; Sampson, 1986b). In support of this idea, Smith (1986) demonstrated that the probability of arrest across neighborhoods declines substantially with increasing socioeconomic status, independent of crime type and other correlates of arrest decisions.

Recent studies have addressed the official data problem in two ways. First they have often limited the domain of crimes to homicide and robbery where police biases are believed to be minimal. A great deal of research shows that for serious crimes, police bias and underreporting are quite minimal or unrelated to community variables of interest (Gove et al., 1985). Second, in the last 20 years self-report and victimization data have been compared to official statistics with concerning to validity issues (Hindelang et al., 1981). Community estimates of crime relying on self-reports have been utilized in a few studies. More commonly, victimization surveys have been used to provide an alternative view from which to view the ecological correlates of crime and delinquency (Sampson, 1990).

Sampson and Lauritsen (1994) note that for serious offenses such as homicide and aggravated assault, offenders tend to commit offenses close to their homes (Brantingham and Brantingham, 1984). They argue that victimization occurrence rates and official offense or arrest rates, particularly at the city level, are tapping the same general dimension with respect to violence. In fact, Sampson and Lauritsen (1994) state there has been a general convergence of neighborhood-level findings between official police statistics and victimization data.

Another problem stems from the lack of relevant data. Heitgard and Bursik (1987) state that traditional ecological studies are not well suited to an examination of the formal and informal networks hypothesized to link community social structure and crime. This type of research requires extensive and constraining data collection within each neighborhood or community in the analysis.

Most previous macro-level research has relied on census data that rarely provide measures for variables hypothesized to mediate the relationship between community structure and crime (Sampson and Lauritsen, 1994). Other researchers (Maccoby et al., 1958; Kapsis, 1976; Simcha-Fagan and Schwartz, 1986) have examined informal social control as a mediating variable, but have been limited by having only a select number of communities or neighborhoods precluding multivariate analysis. In fact, with the exception of the data from

Baltimore (Taylor et al., 1984), Great Britain (Sampson and Groves, 1989), and the Neighborhood Project with sites in Denver, Chicago, and Philadelphia (Elliott et al., 1997), there have been few if any direct tests of the impact of community social control on crime rates.

Another important concept that has often been ignored is the definition and conceptualization of neighborhoods themselves. The vast majority of previous macro-level research use census tracts or census blocks as a representation of community or neighborhood. Census tracts may or may not correspond to social patterns of interaction and cohesion, and they may or may not reflect resident perceptions of neighborhood or community boundaries. Researchers use census tracts or blocks to define neighborhoods because census data describing structural characteristics are convenient and readily available. It is a methodological challenge to define neighborhoods utilizing any other process and developing macro level measures for each neighborhood. However, if we are to understand community or neighborhood influences on crime we will have to develop better conceptual definitions of neighborhoods.

The primary implication of Sampson and Lauritsen's (1994) review on criminological research on violence is the need for contextual analysis where information on neighborhoods or communities are combined with individual-level data to explain crime. Contextual analysis permits examination of the main effects of community structure on individual behavior and also the interaction between community and individual characteristics. Most previous research on crime involves the study of either individual effects or community-level effects. Almost no research has examined both (Reiss, 1986; Gottfredson and Taylor, 1986). Sampson and Lauritsen specifically note that multi-level hierarchical modeling is appealing as a statistical technique to address this limitation.

CHAPTER 4

Methodology

INTRODUCTION

The primary purpose of this research was to conduct a test of Bursik and Grasmick's systemic theory of neighborhood control. Secondary data (Taylor's "Crime Changes in Baltimore, 1970-1994" study) were used to test Bursik and Grasmick's theory. This dataset was recently published by the Inter-university Consortium for Political and Social Research and has some unique characteristics that made it well suited for this purpose.

Conducting a test of a theory that has neighborhoods as a unit of analysis requires data that until recently have not been widely available to researchers. Data needed to test this theory would have to be acquired from a random sample of as large a number of neighborhoods as possible. Individuals within those neighborhoods would have to be surveyed. Outcome measures of crime such as official crime rates or fear of crime reports from survey data would have to be gathered. This type of data is expensive and time consuming to gather. There are only a handful of studies in existence that meet these requirements and "Crime Changes in Baltimore" is one of those studies.

CRIME CHANGES IN BALTIMORE DATA

The Crime Changes in Baltimore data were collected to examine the relationships among crime rates, residents' attitudes, physical deterioration, and neighborhood structure in selected urban Baltimore neighborhoods. The data include both neighborhood-block information and individual-level information for two time periods, 1981-1982 and 1994. The original 1981-1982 study was designed to model neighborhood-level responses to disorder. The purpose of the 1994 study was to see how residents' reactions to crime had changed between 1982 and 1994, and if either neighborhood-perceived incivilities, or neighborhood-assessed incivilities in 1982 helped predict changes in residents' reactions to crime between 1982 and 1994 (Taylor, 1998).

One important element of the Taylor data, which makes it unique from other neighborhood-level datasets examined, concerns the conceptualization of neighborhood. As mentioned in the literature review, most previous macro-level studies utilize census tracts or blocks as an approximation of neighborhood.

Taylor and associates (1979) in collaboration with the Baltimore City Planning Department personnel empirically derived neighborhood units. This procedure relied largely on existing community organization boundaries to define neighborhoods. Neighborhood organization leaders and survey respondents were shown maps of neighborhood boundaries and asked if they agreed with the boundaries and the name of the neighborhood.

Subsequent checks on the reliability and external validity of their procedure confirmed the accuracy of their mapping procedure. In fact, their mapping was used as the basis for the 1980 Neighborhood Statistics Program for

Baltimore City, carried out by the Bureau of Census. Thus, Taylor's data contains conceptually meaningful neighborhood boundaries.

The block level files used for this research include information about crime rates and census data[8]. The crime rate data consist of yearly Part I index crimes (aggravated assault, burglary, homicide, larceny, auto theft, rape, and robbery) obtained from the Baltimore Police Department for all of Baltimore's 236 ecologically-defined neighborhoods, as well as end-of-decade crime rates and percentiles (Taylor, 1998) (See Table 2).

It was hoped that official crime rates could be supplemented with victimization data. However, there were few measures of victimization in the survey data. These include: 1) "in the last year, have you or someone you know in your neighborhood had a problem with people making too much noise?" and 2) "in the last year, has there been a burglary in your home or the home of someone you know in the neighborhood?" None of these measures included violent crime. Thus, official crime rates were used for this study because they are the best measure of crime available.

The problem of using official statistics was mentioned in the literature review. The primary concern is that poor urban neighborhoods may have higher crime rates in part because of greater police concentration compared to higher status neighborhoods.[9]

---

[8] Taylor also collected block level data concerning land use, people counts, and signs of disorder.

[9] Other problems include: 1) many crimes go unreported; 2) police reports may vary in accuracy; 3) sometimes uncompleted crimes are grouped together with completed acts; 4) differences exist among jurisdictions on legal definitions of crimes; 5) it has been suggested that police departments may deliberately alter reported crimes for political support; and 6) police efficiency and improved record keeping may lead to invalid increases in the crime rate (Savitz, 1998).

Table 2: Sources of Data from the Dataset

	Census Data (Block Level)	Crime Data (Block Level)	Survey Data (Individual Level)
Crime Rates		√	
Fear of Crime			√
Socio-economic Composition	√		
Residential Stability	√		
Racial Ethnic Heterogeneity	√		
Primary Relationships			√
Secondary Relationships			√
Public Controls			√
Disorder			√
Parochial Controls			√

Census block characteristics from the 1970, 1980, and 1990 United States Censuses were also present within the dataset. Census data provided neighborhood-level measures of structural characteristics important to Bursik and Grasmick's (1993) theory. Those concepts again are socioeconomic composition, residential stability, and racial heterogeneity. (Taylor, 1998).

The individual-level data files contain surveys of residents in 1982. The 1982 interviews were administered using CATI (computer-aided telephone interviewing). The 1981-82 surveys of residents ask respondents about different aspects of their neighborhoods, such as physical appearance, problems, and crime control, and fear of crime, as well as the respondents' level of satisfaction with and involvement in their neighborhoods. Demographic information was also provided from these surveys (Taylor, 1998).

Sample

In 1981, sixty-six neighborhoods were randomly sampled from the 236 neighborhoods in Baltimore for block assessment. In 1982, households on these blocks were selected for the resident survey through multistage random sampling. In 1994, thirty neighborhoods from each of the sixty-six chosen in 1981 were selected using stratified sampling to maximize the variation on changes in crime between the two research periods.

The sample for this research included sixty-six neighborhoods selected by multistage random sampling in 1982, as discussed above. These neighborhoods were the unit of analysis for the regression models and were the level-two or macro-level measures for the hierarchical linear analysis discussed later in this chapter. There were 1622 cases of individuals sampled from within those sixty-six neighborhoods whose responses constituted individual-level data. These cases were aggregated to the neighborhood-level for the regression analysis and were the level-one or micro-level measures for the hierarchical linear analysis.

Bursik and Grasmick's Theory and the Level of Measurement Problem

Bursik and Grasmick's systemic neighborhood control theory is an attempt to explain crime only at the neighborhood level. Thus, the unit of analysis is neighborhoods and not individuals. The problem is that the data utilized in this study contain measures at both the neighborhood and individual level. Simply adding or averaging individual responses on measures of neighborhood interaction and neighborhood control does not accurately reflect macro-level concepts.

This problem has been examined from the standpoint of what has been termed "aggregation bias". Bursik and Grasmick define aggregation bias as a statistical problem where the findings that result from a statistical analysis are partly dependent on the size of the unit of analysis that is used. They refer to a paper by William Bailey (1985).

Bailey used a single dataset, recoded it to represent the crime rates in U.S. states, Standard Metropolitan Statistical Areas (SMSA's), and cities, and examined the social, demographic, and economic correlates of those crime rates. Very different patterns emerged among the three different levels of analysis, including actual changes in the direction of the relationships. Bailey concluded that the appropriate level of analysis could only be determined by theory.

Blalock (1979), states that there are circumstances when aggregation is quite legitimate. He states "that if one adheres to the extreme position that *no* simple aggregation makes sense, then we will have great difficulty in arriving at criteria that allow us to examine relationships across different levels of analysis (p. 11)." Like Bailey, the critical point by Blalock is that an explicit theoretical model is necessary in order to justify whatever aggregation procedure is used. The more explicit the theory, the easier it will be to criticize and improve upon the measurement of macro-level measures.

In view of the unresolved statistical issues, this research tested the research models using both Ordinary Least Squares Regression and Hierarchical Linear Modeling. Regression allowed for a test of the theory using neighborhoods as a unit of analysis, as the theory suggests.

Because the "Crime Changes in Baltimore" data have a hierarchical structure, (individuals nested within neighborhoods), Hierarchical Linear Analysis (HLM) was used to compare within-neighborhood effects to between neighborhood effects. Also, HLM is a statistical method that helps resolve the problem of aggregation bias. This will be explored in more detail later.

ANALYSIS PLAN

Before testing of the hypotheses in causal analysis, several steps had to be taken. The first step was to manage missing data. Missing data were replaced with the average score of the variable, as long as the percentage of the data representing that variable did not exceed ten percent. If missing data did exceed ten percent for any of the variables than that variable was eliminated from the analysis. The alternative results in loss of cases, which had to be avoided because of the relatively small number of cases available here (Hair et al., 1995, make several useful suggestions concerning missing data).

The second step involved operationalizing the concepts for the analyses. All of the concepts in the models to be tested were represented by scales. Again, this is a useful procedure to reduce the number of variables when the sample size is modest. The scales were developed by adding the individual items together. Confirmatory principle components analysis was used to derive scales and to confirm that individual variables loaded sufficiently on single dimensions. Thus, it was possible to assess the separate relative contributions of all the items to the scales and the internal consistency of the scales. Cronbach's alpha was used to assess the reliability of each scale.

The third step in the analysis plan was to conduct descriptive analyses including; variable frequencies, means, standard deviations, and zero-order correlations.

Descriptive data analysis allows a researcher to develop an understanding of the data and be confident that the variables are appropriate for the planned analysis. Zero-order correlations allowed for an examination of the interrelationships among all variables, checking in particular for multicollinearity among nondependent variables. The final stage of the data analysis involved actually testing the research models. This was done with Ordinary Least Squares (OLS) Regression and Hierarchical Liner Modeling (HLM).

OLS Regression was used to test the model with neighborhoods as the only unit of analysis (with individual-level data aggregated). Because there were only sixty-six neighborhoods in the sample, sample size was a concern in this analysis. A sample of this size would not allow for the introduction of large numbers of variables. Principle components factor analysis aided in the selection of which variables were included to best represent these concepts. Because the purpose of this study is to actually test a theory, confirmatory analysis was the approach used in principle components analysis. Confirmatory analysis is where the analyst completely specifies the variables to be included rather than use a sequential search approach (Hair et al., 1995).

Hierarchical Linear Analysis (HLM) was also used to test the research models. This approach allowed for the use of both neighborhood-level and individual-level measures. The purpose and procedures for using HLM will be described in more detail after a review of how the concepts in Bursik and Grasmick's theory were operationalized.

OPERATIONALIZATION OF CONCEPTS

One of the primary aims of this research was to attempt to develop valid and reliable measures of the key concepts in Bursik and Grasmick's theory. While this theory had not been previously tested, many of the concepts had been measured in other community-level studies (Covington and Taylor, 1991; Sampson and Groves, 1989; Skogan, 1990).

This section discusses the operationalization of the variables in Bursik and Grasmick's model for this dissertation. Table 3 summarizes the variables used in the research model. Component items constituting the variables socioeconomic composition, residential stability, racial and ethnic heterogeneity, primary relationships, secondary relationships, parochial controls, public controls, disorder, crime, and fear of crime are presented in sequential tables.

Measurement of Independent Variables

Socioeconomic Composition
Socioeconomic composition refers to the economic structure of a neighborhood as defined by Bursik and Grasmick. A disadvantaged social structure is theorized to lead to increased residential instability and increased ethnic and racial heterogeneity.

Measures of socioeconomic status were developed from census data (See Table 3). Taylor (1998) gathered census data for all Baltimore neighborhoods in 1970, 1980, and 1990. Census data for 1980 were used in this study. Measures of socioeconomic status include percentage of neighborhood residents that do not own a house, percent of the population that is at or below the poverty line, and percentage of people in the neighborhood without a high school education.

Of the sample of 66 Baltimore neighborhoods, there was wide variation in the percentage of people that do not own a house, that are below the 1980 poverty line, and percentage of the neighborhood that was African American (See Table 4). The mean percentage of people who did not

Table 3: Operationalization and Measurement of Concepts

Variables	Measurement	Source
X1 Socioeconomic Composition (Independent Variable)	Percent that do not own a house, percent below poverty, and percent without a high school education (See Table 4).	Census
X2 Residential Stability (Independent Variable)	Percent change in population in a neighborhood from 1970 to 1980 (See Table 4).	Census
X3 Racial/Ethnic Heterogeneity (Independent Variable)	Percent of the neighborhood population that is African American (See Table 4).	Census
X4 Disorder (Independent Variable)	Perceptions of how problematic a variety of disorders are in the neighborhood (See Table 6).	Survey
X5 Primary Relationships (Intervening Variable)	The number of family (outside the home) and friends that live in the neighborhood (See Table 8).	Survey

Table 3 (Continued): Operationalization and Measurement of Concepts

Variables	Measurement	Measurement Source
X6 Secondary Relationships (Intervening Variable)	Perception of extent and quality of neighborhood interaction (See Table 10).	Survey
X7 Parochial Control (Independent Variable)	Perception of what neighbors would do to confront crime problems in the neighborhood (See Table 12).	Survey
X8 Public Control (Independent Variable)	Perception of whether police would respond to neighborhood crime problems (See Table 13).	Survey
X9 Crime Rate (Dependent Variable)	Personal and property crime rates per 1000 population for the year 1982 (See Table 15).	Baltimore Police Department Records
X10 Fear of Crime (Dependent Variable)	Perception of safety when outside at night and during the day (See Table 17).	Survey

Table 4: Original Component Items of SES, Residential Stability, and Racial Heterogeneity

Item	Mean	S.D. *	Range
Socioeconomic Composition			
Percent of the neighborhood population in 1980 that does not own a house.	45.4	21.4	82.9
Percent of the neighborhood population in 1980 that is at or below the poverty level.	16.5	13.9	58.2
Percent of the neighborhood population in 1980 without a high school education.	26.8	7.1	27.8
Residential Stability			
Percentage of the neighborhood population that changed from 1970 to 1980.	18.9	15.2	93
Racial Concentration			
Percentage of the neighborhood population that is African American	44.1	40.2	99.5

*S.D. = Standard Deviation

own a house was forty-five percent, with a range between eleven and ninety-four percent. The mean percentage of people below poverty was sixteen percent, with a range between one and sixty percent. The mean percentage of people without a high school education was twenty-seven percent, with a range between thirteen and forty percent (See Table 4).

Coefficient alpha was computed to insure internal consistency and reliability in the measure (See Table 5). Coefficient alpha for the socioeconomic status scale was

Table 5: Factor and Reliability Analysis for Socioeconomic Composition

Item	Eigen-value	% of Variance	Factor Loading	Alpha
	2.05	68.5		.77
Percent of the neighborhood population in 1980 that does not own a house.			.80	
Percent of the neighborhood population in 1980 that is at or below the poverty level.			.88	
Percent of the neighborhood population in 1980 without a high school education.			.81	

77, which is over the .70 alpha recommended for a scale to demonstrate internal consistency (Carmines and Zeller, 1979).

Principle components analysis was then conducted to confirm that the three items loaded on a single factor. The Kaiser-Meyer-Olkin Measure of Sampling Adequacy was .67, indicating a good distribution of values for conducting factor analysis (Hair et al.,1995).

The Bartlett Test of Sphericity provides the statistical probability that a correlation matrix has significant correlations among at least some of the variables and is therefore appropriate for factor analysis (Hair et al, 1995). The Bartlett Test of Sphericity in this case was 958.99 (p <.001). Factor loadings should be at least .30 to consider that an item loads on any factor (Carmines and Zeller, 1979). Individual loadings for the socioeconomic status scale ranged from .80 to .88, with an eigenvalue of 2.05, explaining 68.5 percent of the variance in the items (See Table 5).

Residential Stability

Residential stability in Bursik and Grasmick's theory refers to the amount of change in the population level of a neighborhood. Stability in the neighborhood is theorized to lead to more primary and secondary ties in a neighborhood, which in turn leads to greater neighborhood social control. It is measured here as the change in the percentage of the population in a neighborhood from 1970 to 1980.
There was also great variability in change in neighborhood population in the sample of neighborhoods. The range in percent population change was zero to ninety-four percent, with a mean of twenty-three percent.

Racial/Ethnic Heterogeneity

Racial and ethnic heterogeneity refers to the diversity of a neighborhood in terms of racial and ethnic composition. Heterogeneity is expected to impede communication between residents and therefore limit the quality and number of primary and secondary ties in a neighborhood. It is measured as percent of the neighborhood population that is African American. This is an imperfect measure. One would hope for a diversity measure that takes into account other ethnic and racial populations, but those measures were not available in the data.[10]

Like the other structural variables, there was great diversity in the racial composition of the sample of neighborhoods. Neighborhoods ranged from zero to ninety-nine in percentage of the population that was African American, with a mean of forty-four percent.

Measurement of Intervening Variables

Disorder

Disorder is defined as the violation of norms concerning public behavior. It includes both social and physical disorder (See Table 6). Neighborhoods that have high rates of poverty, population turnover, and racial and ethnic heterogeneity often have high levels of disorder. Disorder is expected to lead to a breakdown in primary and secondary relationships, thereby impacting community control. Measures of physical disorder were derived from the perceptions of survey participants.

Average scores range from .25 to .63. Coefficient alpha for the disorder scale was .87, which is well over the .70 alpha recommended for a scale to demonstrate internal consistency (Carmines and Zeller, 1979) (See Table 7).

Principal components analysis was then conducted to confirm that the eleven items loaded on a single factor. The Kaiser-Meyer-Olkin Measure of Sampling Adequacy was .92, indicating a good distribution of values for conducting principle components analysis.

---

[10] A measure of heterogeneity was developed using a dummy variable. The variable percent African American was coded (0) for the top 25 percent and bottom 25 percent of the distribution and coded (1) for the middle 50 percent of the distribution. There were no significant correlations with any other variables when this was done.

Table 6: Original Component Items Constituting Disorder

How big a problem is ... in your neighborhood (0 = not a problem, 1 = somewhat of a problem, 3 = a big problem)			
Item	**Mean**	**S.D.***	**Range**
Vandalism	0.5	0.7	0-2
Vacant housing	0.3	0.6	0-2
Poor upkeep of property	0.5	0.7	0-2
People insulting other people	0.3	0.6	0-2
Litter in streets	0.5	0.7	0-2
Vacant lots with trash	0.3	0.7	0-2
Groups of teens loitering	0.6	0.8	0-2
Amount of noise	0.6	0.8	0-2
Bad elements moving in	0.3	0.6	0-2
People fighting and arguing	0.3	0.6	0-2

The Bartlett Test of Spericity, a measure of correlations within a correlation matrix, was 5832.5 (p < .001). Individual loadings for the disorder factor ranged from .54 to .72, with an eigenvalue of 4.83, explaining 43.9 percent of the variance in the items. Table 7 displays the factor loading and reliability analysis for the disorder factor.

Primary Relational Networks

Primary relational networks refers to the density of family and friendship networks. Bursik and Grasmick's theory states that when family and friendship networks break down, it is more difficult to maintain neighborhood social control, especially over children. Measures of primary relationships were derived from a composite of the number of family members and friends that live in the respondents' neighborhood (See Table 8).

Table 7: Factor and Reliability Analyses for Disorder

Items	Eigen-value	% of Variance	Factor Loading	Al-pha
	4.83	43.9		0.87
Vandalism			0.61	
Vacant housing			0.54	
Poor upkeep property			0.65	
People insulting…			0.67	
Litter in the streets			0.72	
Vacant lots with trash			0.61	
Groups of teens			0.72	
Amount of noise			0.71	
Bad elements moving in			0.69	
People fighting…			0.72	

Table 8: Original Component Items Constituting Primary Relational Networks

Items	Mean	S.D.	Range
Other than people in your household, how many relatives do you have who live in your neighborhood?	1.1	3.7	0-50
How many friends who are not relatives do you have who live in your neighborhood?	7.8	11.2	0-50

The average number of relatives living in a neighborhood was 1.1 with a range of zero to fifty. The variable number of friends in the neighborhood also ranged from zero to fifty with an average of 7.8.

Coefficient alpha was computed with the two variables. Alpha for family and friendship networks was low (.37) (See Table 9). The value of alpha depends on the average interitem correlation and the number of items in the scale (Carmines and Zeller, 1979). Specifically, as the average correlation among items increases and as the number of items increases, the value of alpha increases. The correlation between family networks and friendship networks was .23; significant at the .001 level but still a rather weak correlation. The somewhat low correlation and the small number of variables resulted in the low alpha value.

Principle components analysis indicated that both items loaded on a single factor. The Kaiser-Meyer-Olkin Measure of Sampling Adequacy was .50, indicating a good distribution of values for conducting principle components analysis. The Bartlett Test of Sphericity was 87.9 (p < .001). The factor loadings for each of the two variables was .78 with an eigenvalue of 1.23, explaining 61.5 percent of the variance in the items. Even though the low alpha value was a concern, it was decided to combine family and friendship networks into one concept on the strength of the results of the principle components analysis and because Bursik and Grasmick specifically define primary relationships as the density of family and friendship networks.

Table 9: Factor Analysis and Reliability Analysis for Primary Relational Networks

Items	Eigen-value	% of Variance	Factor Loading	Al-pha
	1.23	61.5		0.37
Other than people in your household, how many relatives do you have who live in your neighborhood?			0.78	
How many friends who are not relatives do you have who live in your neighborhood?			0.78	

Secondary Relational Networks

Secondary relational networks refer to the degree of neighborhood interaction. It is expected from the theory that neighborhoods with residents that meet regularly feel a sense of identification with the neighborhood, and are willing to watch a neighbor's property, which will lead to a more cohesive neighborhood. Strong secondary relational networks are expected to lead to a greater ability to impose neighborhood social control. Measures of secondary relational networks are presented in Table 10.

Average scores ranged from .2 to .8 for the dichotomous variables. For the variables feel a sense of community and feel responsible for happenings around the corner the average responses were 2.2 and 2.0 respectively. Coefficient alpha for the thirteen items was .72.

Table 10: Original Component Items Constituting Secondary Relationships

Items	Mean	S.D.	Range
Does your neighborhood have a name? *(0 = no, 1 = yes)*	0.8	0.4	0-1
Do you feel a sense of community with others in the neighborhood? *(1 = not at all, 2 = somewhat, 3 = a great deal)*	2.2	0.7	0-3
Do you feel responsible for happenings around the corner in your neighborhood? *(1 = no, 2 = some, 3 = big responsibility)*	2.0	0.7	0-3
In the past year, have you run an errand for a neighbor on the block? *(0 = no, 1 = yes)*	0.6	0.5	0-1
Have you visited inside a neighbor's house on the block? *(0 = no, 1 = yes)*	0.8	0.4	0-1
Have you argued with a neighbor on your block? *(0 = no, 1 = yes)*	0.2	0.4	0-1
Have you borrowed an item from a neighbor on your block? *(0 = no, 1 = yes)*	0.5	0.5	0-1
Have you worked with neighbors to improve block appearance? *(0 = no, 1 = yes)*	0.5	0.5	0-1

However, principle components analysis indicated that the items did not load on a single factor. The items loaded on four separate factors. The first factor consisted of the last three items; while away neighbors watch your house, neighbors care for mail, and neighbors have your key (or

Table 10 (Continued): Original Component Items Constituting Secondary Relationships

Items	Mean	S.D.	Range
Have you tried to stop a neighbor's child from doing something they shouldn't be doing? *(0 = no, 1 = yes)*	0.5	0.5	0-1
In your neighborhood, do neighbors get together about neighborhood problems? *(0 = no, 1 = yes)*	0.3	0.4	0-1
Have you kept watch on a house or apartment while a neighbor was away, or has a neighbor done this for you? *(0 = no, 1 = yes)*	0.2	0.4	0-3
Have you arranged with other people in your neighborhood to have newspapers or mail brought in while your away? *(0 = no, 1 = yes)*	0.3	0.5	0-3
Have you given another person in your neighborhood your key, or have they given you theirs, so that animals could be fed, plants watered, or the house checked on while your away? *(0 = no, 1 = yes)*	0.4	0.5	0-1

you do the same for them). The factor loadings were all high, ranging from .74 to .82 with an eigenvalue of 3.30, explaining 25.4 percent of the variance in the items. Coefficient alpha for these three items was .72 (See Table 11).

Table 11: Factor and Reliability Analysis for Secondary Relationships

Item	Eigen-value	% of Variance	Factor Loading	Al-pha
	1.93	64.3		0.72
Have you kept watch on a house or apartment while a neighbor was away, or has a neighbor done this for you?			0.79	
Have you kept watch on a house or apartment while a neighbor was away, or has a neighbor done this for you?			0.84	
Have you given another person in your neighborhood your key			0.77	

The second factor consisted of six items including: in the past year ran an errand for a neighbor, visited inside a neighbor's house, argued with a neighbor, worked to improve neighborhood appearance, tried to stop neighbor's child from doing wrong, and neighbors got together informally about problems.

The factor loadings for these items ranged from .42 to .64 with an eigenvalue of 1.30, explaining 10 percent of the variance in the items. Coefficient alpha for these six items was .59.

The third factor consisted of two items; feel a sense of community and feel responsible for happenings around the corner. These items had factor loadings of .74 and .70 respectively, with an eigenvalue of 1.13, explaining 8.7 percent of the variance in the items. Coefficient alpha for the items was .48.

The fourth factor also consisted of two items; does your neighborhood have a name and in the past year have you borrowed something from a neighbor. These items had factor loadings of .83 and .45 respectively, with an eigenvalue of 1.01, explaining 7.7 percent of the variance in the items. Coefficient alpha for the two items was .22.

It was decided to develop a measure of secondary relational networks from the first factor only. Both of the first two factors to be extracted from the analysis measured dimensions of secondary relational networks (See Table 11 above). The second factor seemed to identify the extent of interaction with neighbors, which is consistent with Bursik and Grasmick's definition of the concept secondary relational networks.

While the second factor represents extent of neighborhood interaction, the first factor seems to represent quality of neighborhood interaction. Allowing a neighbor to watch over your house while away and keep your keys implies a level of trust and commitment that the second factor does not capture. The first factor is also more internally reliable (.72 alpha compared to .59). Principle components analysis was conducted again on the remaining items.

Parochial Control

Secondary networks refer to the degree of neighborhood interaction. Parochial control on the other hand refers to actual neighborhood social control. It refers to activities that neighborhoods might actually implement to control the behavior of fellow residents or outsiders to the neighborhood. From Bursik and Grasmick's theory, it is expected that parochial control will lead to lower crime rates and to fear of crime. Measures of parochial control were developed from an index of responses to questions concerning what neighbors would do when confronted with various crime related problems (See Table 12).

Unfortunately, there was a problem with missing data with the measures of parochial control. Over ten percent of the cases were missing from the following variables: would neighbors get other neighbors help to stop kids from spray painting, would your neighbor try to stop a person from breaking into a neighbor's home, would they get other neighbor's to help stop the burglar, and do you think neighbors would get neighbor's help to stop teens from making noise.

It was decided not to use the variables that had a large percentage of missing data, thus five variables remained. Average scores ranged from .7 to .9 for the dichotomous variables. Coefficient alpha for the parochial social control scale was .54, less than the alpha recommended to demonstrate internal consistency.

The scale items for the parochial control concept were to be derived from essentially three vignettes. Respondents are asked how they and their neighbors would respond to three different confrontations with deviance in their neighborhood; tell the intruders to stop, get a neighbor's help, and/or call the police. The variables with missing data disrupted the continuity of these items. The internal consistency of the measure of this concept would likely be much stronger if not for the removal of the four variables, and the scale would likely be stronger.

Because of the measurement problems with parochial control, it was decided to combine the variables constituting parochial and public control to determine whether the combined measures would increase the reliability of the scale (See Table 13 for Measures of Public

Table 12: Original Component Items Constituting Parochial Control

Item	Mean	S.D.	Range
Suppose some kids were spray painting a building on your street. Do you think any of your neighbors would tell them to stop? *(0 = no, 1 = yes)*	0.9	0.3	0-1
Do you think any of your neighbors would get another neighbor's help to stop the kids from spray painting? *(0 = no, 1 = yes)*	*		
Do you think any of your neighbors would call the police? *(0 = no, 1 = yes)*	0.9	0.2	0-1
Suppose a suspicious person was trying to break into a neighbor's home. Do you think any of your neighbors would personally try to stop the person? *(0 = no, 1 = yes)*	*		
Do you think any of your neighbors would get another neighbor's help to try to stop the person from breaking into the house? *(0 = no, 1 = yes)*	*		
Do you think any of your neighbors would call the police? *(0 = no, 1 = yes)*	0.9	0.1	0-1

*Variable dropped due to missing data > 10%.

Table 12 (Continued): Original Component Items Constituting Parochial Control

Item	Mean	S.D.	Range
Suppose some teenagers around 15 or 16 years old were shouting and making a loud disturbance on your street around 11:00 at night. Do you think any of your neighbors would tell them to stop? *(0 = no, 1 = yes)*	0.7	0.4	0-1
Do you think any of our neighbors would get another neighbor's help to stop the teenagers from making noise? *(0 = no, 1 = yes)*	*		
Do you think any of your neighbors would call the police? *(0 = no, 1 = yes)*	0.8	0.3	0-1

*Variable dropped due to missing data > 10%.

Control). It did increase the reliability of the scale considerably. The reliability and principle components analysis for the combined parochial/public control scale will be discussed below.

It would not make sense conceptually to combine these measures if public control were measured as intended; the ability of a neighborhood to obtain public goods and services. Those types of measures were unavailable. Public control was measured using an index of residents' perceptions of whether the police would respond to the same neighborhood crime problems used for the measures of parochial control. In other words, the measures for public control were derived from the same set of questions as those of parochial control (See Table 12).

Public Control

Bursik and Grasmick defined public control as the ability of a community to obtain public goods and services from agencies outside the community. These goods and services include health care, social services, and policing. It could also include funding from public agencies for crime control programs. The ability to obtain support from outside the community concerning crime control is expected to impact the level of crime and fear of crime in a neighborhood.

Taylor and associates did ask survey questions concerning whether the respondent was involved in an organization that had been involved in providing jobs and job training for youth, putting pressure on landlords or the city to improve property, and trying to get better police services.

Unfortunately, there were too many missing data from these items. Taylor did not include these variables in the published data for this reason. Thus, the data only allow us to tap into the one dimension of public control; whether police would respond if called to a variety of disturbances (See Table 13).

Coefficient alpha for the combined parochial/public control scale was .73, indicating internal consistency among the items. Principle components analysis confirmed that the items loaded on one factor. Kaiser-Meyer-Olkin Measure of Sampling Adequacy was .76, indicating a good distribution of values for conducting principle components analysis. The Bartlett Test of Sphericity was 2473 (p < .001). The factor loadings ranged from .46 to .78 with an eigenvalue of 2.85, explaining 35.6 percent of the variance in the items (See Table 14).

Table 13: Original Component Items Constituting Public Control

Items	Mean	S.D.	Range
Suppose some kids were spray painting a building on your street. Do you think the police would come and do something about it? *(0 = no, 1= yes)*	0.9	0.2	0-1
Suppose a suspicious person was trying to break into a neighbor's home and your neighbors called the police, do you think the police would come and do something about it? *(0 = no, 1 = yes)*	0.9	0.3	0-1
Suppose some teenagers around 15 or 16 years old were shouting and making a loud disturbance on your street around 11:00 at night and your neighbors called the police, do you think the police would come and do something about it? *(0 = no, 1 = yes)*	0.9	0.3	0-1

Table 14: Factor Analysis and Reliability Analysis for Parochial/Public Control

Items	Eigen-value	% of Variance	Factor Loading	Alpha
	2.85	35.6		.73
Teen vandalism- do you think your neighbors would tell them to stop?			0.48	
Teen vandalism- do you think your neighbors would call the police?			0.51	
Teen vandalism- do you think the police would come and do something about it?			0.77	
Burglary- do you think any of your neighbors would call the police?			0.47	
Burglary- do you think the police would come and do anything about it?			0.65	
Teens disturbance- do you think your neighbors would tell them to stop?			0.46	
Teen disturbance- do you think your neighbors would call the police?			0.55	
Teen disturbance- do you think the police would come and do something about it?			0.78	

Dependent Variables

There are two dependent variables in this study; crime rates and fear of crime. Separate models will be estimated for each dependent variable. Bursik and Grasmick make it clear that their theory best explains crime in which there is widespread consensus. They refer to the index crimes in the Uniform Crime Reports as an appropriate measure. A measure of crime rates for each neighborhood was developed using the index offenses; homicide, rape, robbery, burglary, motor vehicle theft, and larceny (See Table 15).

<u>Crime Rates</u>

Frequency measures of 1982 crime rates indicate that there was a great deal of variation in the level of crime reported to the police among the sixty-six sampled neighborhoods (See Table 15). The average homicide rate for the sampled Baltimore neighborhoods per 1000 population was 26.7. The homicide rate ranged between zero in thirty-three neighborhoods to 174 in one neighborhood. The average rape rate per 1000 population was 71.6 with a range between zero in eight neighborhoods to 364 in one neighborhood. The robbery rate varied widely from forty-four to 4679 per 1000 population. The average robbery rate was 1385.8. The average rate of assaults per 1000 population was 809 with a range between thirty-five and 3077. The average larceny rate was 4776.9 with a range from 1240 to 20,545 in the sixty-six Baltimore neighborhoods. The average burglary rate was 2597.8 with a range between 332 and 10389. The average auto theft rate was 664.9 per 1000 population with a range between 44 and 2347.

Table 15: Original Component Items Constituting Crime Rates

Items	Mean	S.D.	Range
Homicide rate per 1000 population in 1982	26.7	39.3	174
Rape rate per 1000 population in 1982	71.6	75.5	364
Robbery rate per 1000 population in 1982	1385.8	1267.5	4635
Assault rate per 1000 population in 1982	809	688.1	3042
Larceny rate per 1000 population in 1982	4776.9	3333.3	19,305
Burglary rate per 1000 population in 1982	2597.8	1843.3	10,057
Auto theft rate per 1000 population in 1982	664.9	428.8	2303

Coefficient alpha for the crime rate scale was .86, which is over the recommended alpha for internal consistency of a scale (Carmines and Zeller, 1979) (See Table 16). Principle components analysis indicated that all the items loaded on one factor. The Kaiser-Meyer-Olkin Measure of Sampling Adequacy was .79, indicating a good distribution of values for conducting principle components analysis. The Bartlett Test of Sphericity was 219.3 ($p <$ .001). The factor loadings ranged from .56 to .86 with an eigenvalue of 3.915, explaining 55.9 percent of the variance in the seven items.

Table 16: Factor and Reliability Analysis for Crime Rates

Items	Eigen-value	% of Variance	Factor Loading	Alph a
Homicide rate per 1000 population in 1982	3.92	55.9		0.86
Rape rate per 1000 population in 1982			0.56	
Robbery rate per 1000 population in 1982			0.74	
Assault rate per 1000 population in 1982			0.85	
Larceny rate per 1000 population in 1982			0.74	
Burglary rate per 1000 population in 1982			0.81	
Auto theft rate per 1000 population in 1982			0.86	
Homicide rate per 1000 population in 1982			0.62	

Fear of Crime

Bursik and Grasmick define fear of crime as an emotional response to fear provoking stimuli in the neighborhood. A measure of this concept was developed from survey responses concerning how fearful the respondent would be walking in their neighborhood at night and also during the day (See Table 17).

Table 17: Original Component Items Constituting Fear of Crime

How safe would you feel ... ? (1 = very safe, 2 = somewhat safe, 3 = somewhat unsafe, 4 = very unsafe)			
Items	**Mean**	**S.D.**	**Range**
being alone in your neighborhood during the day	1.4	0.7	1-4
if you were out alone at night	2.3	1.1	1-4
being alone on your block during the day	1.2	0.5	1-4
if you were out alone on your block at night	1.9	1.0	1-4

Average scores range from 1.2 to 2.3. Coefficient alpha for the fear of crime scale was .81, demonstrating internal consistency among the four items (See Table 18). Principle components analysis indicated that the items loaded on one factor. The Kaiser- Meyer-Olkin Measure of Sampling Adequacy was .68, indicating a good distribution of values for conducting principle components analysis. The Bartlett Test of Sphericity, a statistical test for significant correlations among the items, was 2538.2 (p < .001).

The factor loadings ranged from .77 to .82 with an eigenvalue of 2.59, explaining 64.7 percent of the variance in the four items (See Table 18).

This chapter has presented all the concepts represented in this study, how these concepts are addressed by Bursik and Grasmick, and how they are operationalized for this research. Frequencies, means, standard deviations, reliability analyses, and principle components analyses have been presented where appropriate. Limitations of some of these measures have also been presented.

Table 18: Factor Reliability Analysis for Fear of Crime

Item	Eigen-value	% of Variance	Factor Loading	Alpha
How safe would you feel...	2.59	64.7		0.82
being alone in your neighborhood during the day			0.82	
if you were out alone at night			0.81	
being alone on your block during the day			0.77	
if you were out alone on your block at night			0.82	

Chapter 5 presents bivariate and multivariate analyses of the variables in the research models. The results of the analyses by Ordinary Least Squares Regression and Hierarchical Linear Modeling on the dependent variables crime rates and fear of crime are discussed. Hypotheses stated in Chapter 2 that were derived from Bursik and Grasmick's theory are repeated along with specific findings.

HIERARCHICAL LINEAR MODELING

The research models depicted in figures two through five will be tested using hierarchical linear modeling (HLM). Bursik and Grasmick's theory is a linear model that contains concepts at two different units of analysis. Social structure and setting are measured at the neighborhood-level while the intervening variables are measured at the individual level. Thus, these data have a hierarchical structure with individuals nested within neighborhoods. With hierarchical linear models, each of the levels in this structure is formally represented by its own submodel. These submodels express relationships among variables within a given level, and specify how variables at one level influence relations occurring at another (Bryk and Raudenbush, 1992).

Many questions about how organizations (in this case neighborhoods) affect the individuals within them can be formulated as two-level hierarchical linear models. At level one, the units are persons and each person's outcome is represented as a function of a set of individual characteristics. At level two, the units are organizations. The regression coefficients in the Level-1 model for each organization are conceived as outcome variables that are hypothesized to depend on specific organizational characteristics (Bryk and Raudenbush, 1992).

A number of conceptual and statistical difficulties have plagued past analyses of multilevel data in criminological research. Among the most commonly encountered difficulties have been aggregation bias, misestimated standard errors, and heterogeneity of regression (Bryk and Raudenbush, 1992).

Aggregation bias can occur when a variable takes on different meanings and therefore may have different effects at different levels of analysis. In criminology research, for example, the average social class of a neighborhood may have an effect on friendship networks or organizational participation above and beyond the effect of the individual respondent's social class. Hierarchical linear models help resolve this confounding by facilitating a decomposition of any observed relationship between variables, such as organizational participation and social class, into separate Level-1 and Level-2 components (Bryk and Raudenbush, 1992).

Misestimated standard errors occur with multilevel data when we fail to take into account the dependence among individual responses within the same organization. This dependence may arise because of shared experiences within the organization, because of the ways in which individuals were initially drawn into the organization, or in how a researcher defines the boundary of the group of interest. Hierarchical linear models resolve this problem by incorporating into the statistical model a unique random effect for each organizational unit. The variability in these random effects is taken into account in estimating standard errors. In survey research, these standard error estimates adjust for the intraclass correlation, or the design effect that occurs as a result of cluster sampling (Bryk and Raudenbush, 1992).

Heterogeneity of regression occurs when the relationships between individual characteristics and outcomes vary across organizations. Hierarchical linear models enable the investigator to estimate a separate set of regression coefficients for each organizational unit, and then to model variation among the organizations in their sets of coefficients as multivariate outcomes to be explained by organizational factors. Burnstein (1980) provides a review of this notion.

In sum, despite the prevalence of hierarchical structures in criminological theories and research, past studies have often failed to address them adequately in the data analysis. This neglect has largely reflected limitations in conventional statistical techniques such as multiple ordinary least squares regression and structural equation modeling techniques for the estimation of linear models with nested structures. In social research, these limitations have generated concerns about aggregation bias, misestimated standard errors, and heterogeneity of regression (Bryk and Raudenbush, 1992).

These limitations have also fostered an impoverished conceptualization, discouraging the formulation of explicit models with hypotheses about effects occurring at each level and across levels. I used hierarchical linear modeling to test Bursik and Grasmick's theory. The statistical program HLM (Hierarchical Linear Modeling) by Bryk and Raudenbush was used for the analysis.

Because HLM can be used for a variety of purposes, the analyst has several choices in HLM models. The purpose of this study was to develop an understanding of how neighborhood context impacts crime through and independent of individual-level concepts within those organizations. Bryk and Raudenbush (1992) describe how to formulate and test hypotheses about how variables measured at one level affect relations occurring at another. They state that in conducting this type of research, the analyst has several choices in formulating models.

A random-intercept model was used for this study. This type of model allows for an adjustment of the neighborhood-level effect estimates for various characteristics of individuals within the neighborhoods. Statistical adjustment for individual background is important because people are not assigned to neighborhoods at random. Failure to control for background may bias the estimates of neighborhood effects. Also, if the individual-level predictors are strongly related to the dependent variable, controlling for them will increase the precision of the estimates of neighborhood-level effects.

Model specification also involves random versus nonrandom effects. That is, the analyst can specify whether individual-level coefficients vary randomly over the population or whether individual characteristics are assumed to have the same influence on a neighborhood. The random effects model is appropriate for this

Study because we are assuming that there is variation at the individual level of analysis with respect to neighborhoods. Individual-level coefficients are expected to vary with respect to neighborhood-level measures.

HLM will provide a decomposition of individual-level effects and compositional or contextual effects. That is, the technique will provide separate regression coefficients and variance explained statistics for the entire hierarchical analysis, individual-level or within-neighborhood analysis, and neighborhood-level or between-neighborhood analysis. This will give us a picture of the proportionate contribution of the neighborhood-level concepts social structure and setting to the individual-level concepts in Bursik and Grasmick's theory in their explanation of crime.

LIMITATIONS

There are several limitations to this research design that deserve mention. The "Crime Changes in Baltimore" data were not gathered for the purpose of testing this theory. Therefore, measures of some of the variables in Bursik and Grasmick's theory are not ideal. For example, the measures of fear of crime would have been better if they had attempted to measure fear of being the victim of specific offenses. It would have also been beneficial to have measures of personal victimization of violent and nonviolent crimes to compare to the crime rate measures.

Also, only sixty-six neighborhoods are to be utilized in this research with only 1622 individual surveys. Finally, Bursik and Grasmick's theory makes predictions about the effects of changes in community structure over time. While the Baltimore data do have two time periods in which surveys were administered, the number of surveys in 1994 were cut almost in half, making a longitudinal design problematic. Thus, it was decided to use only 1982 measures for all the concepts in the theory.

CHAPTER 5
Findings

INTRODUCTION

This chapter presents the results of analyses of the research models described in Chapter 3. The first model attempts to explain crime rates through Ordinary Least Squares Regression where neighborhood is the unit of analysis for all measures. The second model attempts to explain fear of crime through Ordinary Least Squares Regression where neighborhood is the unit of analysis and by Hierarchical Linear Modeling (HLM) in which the units of analysis are neighborhoods and individuals.

Recall that HLM is appropriate when one has nested data. In this case, individual survey respondents are nested within neighborhoods. HLM can only be applied when the dependent variable is of the same unit of analysis as the lowest level of data (Hox, 1995). Thus, in this case, HLM can only be applied when the dependent variable comes from individual survey responses. The dependent variable, fear of crime, is an individual-level variable derived from survey responses. Crime rate is a neighborhood-level variable derived from the Baltimore Police Department and therefore is inappropriate for HLM analysis. The research hypotheses and findings applying to each model are presented in separate tables at the end of appropriate sections.

MODEL 1: EXPLAINING CRIME RATES

The index of crime rates is a metric level variable. Thus, the appropriate technique for examining the effects of the independent variables on the dependent variables was Ordinary least squares (OLS) regression. OLS regression is a multivariate technique that provides a means of objectively assessing the degree and character of the relationship between dependent and independent variables by forming a variate of independent variables (Hair et al., 1995). The independent variables, in addition to their collective prediction through the dependent variable, may also be considered for their individual contribution to the variate and its predictions. Interpretation of the variate may rely on any of three perspectives: the importance of the independent variables, the types of relationships found, or the interrelationships among the independent variables (Hair et al., 1995).

Parameters of the OLS regression model are estimated using confirmatory specification, wherein the set of independent variables to be included in the analysis are completely specified. That is, unlike sequential search approaches where variables are added or deleted if they do not make a significant contribution to the model, with confirmatory specification the researcher has total control over the variable selection.

Bivariate Analysis

Bivariate patterns of association were examined prior to the multivariate analysis. Table 19 displays a matrix of Pearson product-moment correlation coefficients for the variables in the research model predicting crime rates. As expected, there were strong and significant correlations between crime rates and the independent variables socioeconomic status, percent African American, and population stability. Population stability was the strongest correlate of crime rates (r = .59, p. < .01), followed closely by socioeconomic status (r = .54, p < .01). The association between crime rates and the percentage of the neighborhood population that was African American was not as strong (r = .25, p < .05).

Among the intervening variables, disorder and secondary relational networks were the only variables that had significant correlations with crime rates. Primary relational networks was not statistically significantly correlated with crime rates (r = .17, p = .09)[15]. Parochial and public control were also not significantly associated with crime rates (r = -.15). Disorder was the variable most strongly correlated with crime rates among the intervening variables (r = .40, p < .01). The more that respondents perceived a high level of disorder in their neighborhood, the higher the crime rates.

Secondary relational networks was significantly and negatively associated with crime rates (r = -.33, p < .01). Thus, the more neighbors interact with and trust each other, the lower the crime rate in sampled neighborhoods. On the whole there were strong correlations between crime rates and the independent and intervening variables in the expected direction with the exception of primary relational networks, parochial and public control.

An examination of Table 19 also reveals several variables that are highly correlated (> .40) as is common in aggregate-level analysis. Multicollinearity has substantial effects on regression results. If multicollinearity occurs, it makes determining the contribution of each independent variable impossible because the effects of the independent variables are confounded due to high intercorrelations. High multicollinearity results in larger portions of shared

---

[15] With this sample size it may have been appropriate to use a more liberal alpha level.

Table 19: Correlation Matrix of Variables- Crime Rate Model

	Stability	African American	SES	Disorder	Primary	Secondary	Parochial & Public
African American	.06						
SES	.28*	.40**					
Disorder	.04	.29**	.59**				
Primary	.47**	-.35**	-.03	-.15			
Secondary	.08	-.59**	-.44**	-.58**	.44**		
Paroch & Public	-.14	-.27**	-.41**	.99**	.03	.46**	
Disorder & Secondary	.02	.35**	.60**	.40**	-.20	.68**	-.59**
Crime Rates	.58**	.25**	.54**	.40***	.17	-.33**	-.15

* = p < .05; ** p < .01; ***p < .001

variance and lower levels of unique variance from which the effects of the individual predictor variables can be determined. As a result of multicollinearity regression coefficients may be incorrectly estimated and even have the wrong signs (Hair et al, 1995).

Among the structural variables, socioeconomic status and percent African American were strongly and positively correlated (r = .40, p < .01). Among the aggregated neighborhood variables, disorder was strongly and positively associated with socioeconomic status (r = .59, p < .01), secondary relationships (r = .58, p < .01), and parochial/public control (r = -.58, p < .01). Primary relationships was strongly correlated with population stability (r = .47, p < .01) and secondary relationships (r = .44, p < .01). Secondary relationships was strongly correlated with percent African American (r = -.59, p < .01), socioeconomic status (r = -.44, p < .01), and disorder and primary relational networks, as already mentioned. Parochial and public control was strongly correlated with socioeconomic status (r = -.41, p < .01), and disorder and secondary relationships as already mentioned.

The several high zero-order correlations in a single model, combined with the small sample size (N = 66), made it imperative to address the threat of multicollinearity. A preliminary run of the models without addressing this problem also suggested multicollinearity effects as variables were added to the analysis. The high degree of multicollinearity makes it impractical to run regression analysis without making changes to the research model because it would be difficult to identify the unique contribution of each variable in explaining crime rates. Adjustments to the multivariate models to resolve this problem are discussed in the next section.

Multivariate Analysis

Bursik and Grasmick predict that the structural variables socioeconomic status, residential stability, and racial heterogeneity predict level of crime rates in a neighborhood through disorder, primary and secondary relational networks, and parochial and public control. The interpretation of the total, direct, and indirect effects of individual variables with the full theoretically-derived model for crime rates was impractical due to the high multicollinearity among the independent and intervening variables. Therefore, several steps were taken to address multicollinearity problems, without unduly precluding interpretation of the results as they address the hypotheses.

Hair et al. (1995) suggest several options for researchers encountering multicollinearity problems. First, it is possible to omit one or more highly correlated independent variables from the analysis. Second, a researcher can use the simple correlations between each predictor and the dependent variable to understand the predictor-dependent variable relationship. Berry and Feldman (1985) suggest another option; combine two or more independent variables that are highly correlated into a single variable and use the composite variable in place of the correlated variables in the regression analysis. It was decided to use all three approaches, as they fit conceptual and analytical needs of this research.

First, it was decided to estimate separate regression models for socioeconomic status and percent African American, dropping each of these variables sequentially. The first model includes socioeconomic status but leaves out percent African American due to the high collinearity among these variables (See Table 20). The second model includes percent African American and removes socioeconomic status (See Table 21). It was decided not to combine these two variables into a composite measure because of the importance of the unique concepts to a test of Bursik and Grasmick's theory.

Second, the variables primary relationships and parochial/public control were dropped from the analysis due to their high multicollinearity with the other independent variables, and because neither variable was significantly correlated with crime rates. Interpretation of their importance for crime rates will rely on their zero-order correlation.

Finally, disorder and secondary relational networks were combined into one measure. Both of these concepts were strongly correlated with crime rates and with each other. While combining them loses their separate conceptual effects, the same result would occur if they were left separate. That is, leaving them separate in the analysis would also confound the unique interpretation of each concept in the explanation of crime rates because of the multicollinearity problem.

Normality of the dependent variable is a critical assumption in regression. The variable crime rates was found to be only slightly positively skewed (Skewness = 1.34), thus it was not transformed.

Table 20 presents the results of OLS regression with the revised model of crime rates, using the neighborhood-level structural variables residential stability and socioeconomic status, and the aggregated individual-level variable disorder/secondary relational networks. Percent African American was excluded. The regression model was estimated using confirmatory specification in the total effects model. Thus, the structural variables were entered into the analysis first.

Table 20: Total, Direct, and Indirect Effects of Residential Stability and SES on Crime Rates with Disorder/Secondary Relationships Intervening (OLS) (N = 66)

Independent Variables	Standardized Regression Coefficients		
	Total Effect	Indirect Effect	Direct Effect
Residential Stability	.46***	-.04	.50***
SES	.41***	.16	.25*
Disorder/Secondary Relational Networks			.26*
R-Square	.49***		.53***

*p < .05; ***p < .001

The total effects model was significant in predicting crime rates (p < .001). This model explained 49 percent of the total variance in crime rates. Residential stability was better than socioeconomic status in predicting crime rates (beta = .46, p < .001). The greater the percentage change in population in a neighborhood the higher the crime rate. Socioeconomic status was also significant in its effect on crime rates (beta = .41, p < .001).

In the direct effects model, the combined measure of disorder and secondary relational networks was added. Again, the model was significant in predicting crime rates (p < .001). Addition of the aggregate individual-level variable increased the variance explained from 49 percent to 53 percent. The disorder/secondary relational networks measure had a positive effect on crime rates (beta = .26, p < .001).

The second column in Table 20 reports the indirect effect of residential stability and SES on crime rates, through the individual-level variables disorder/secondary relational networks. This is estimated by subtracting the direct effects of the independent variables from their direct effects (Alwin and Hauser, 1975).

The total effect of one variable on another is the part of their zero-order correlation (total association) which is due neither to their common causes, to correlation among their causes, nor to unanalyzed correlation (Alwin and Hauser, 1975). Indirect effects are those parts of a variable's total effect which are transmitted or mediated by variables specified as intervening between the cause and effect of interest (Alwin and Hauser, 1975). The direct effect of one variable on another is that part of its total effect which is not transmitted via intervening variables. It is the effect which remains when intervening variables are held constant (Alwin and Hauser, 1975).

For population stability, its total effect on crime rates was beta = .46, and its direct effect was beta = .50. Thus, the addition of disorder/secondary relational networks increased the correlation coefficient very slightly (by .04). Thus, the total effect was virtually unchanged.

The regression coefficient for SES in the total effects model was .41 (p < .001). In the direct effect model, the regression coefficient was .25 (p < .05). Thus, of the total effect of SES on crime rates (.41), 39 percent (.41-.25/.41) is mediated by disorder/secondary relational networks, and .25 (61 percent) is unmediated or a direct effect. Sixty-one percent of the total effect (.25/.41) is direct controlling for the intervening variables disorder/secondary relationships.

Table 21 presents the results of OLS regression on crime rates using the same concepts as the previous model except that percent African American replaces socioeconomic status in the model. Again the structural variables were entered into the analysis first. The model was significant in predicting crime rates (p < .001). This model explained 38 percent of the variance in crime rates.

Table 21: Total, Direct, and Indirect Effects of Residential Stability and Percent African American on Crime Rates with Disorder/Secondary Relationships Intervening (OLS) (N = 66)

	Standardized Regression Coefficients		
Independent Variables	**Total Effect**	**Indirect Effect**	**Direct Effect**
Residential Stability	.57***	.01	.56***
African American	.22*	.14	.08
Disorder/Secondary Relational Networks			.37***
R-Square	.38***		.50***

*p < .05; ***p < .001

Examination of the standardized regression coefficients indicates that residential stability was the best predictor of crime rates (beta = .57, p < .001). Percent African American had a smaller but significant effect on crime rates (beta = .22, p < .05).

The disorder/secondary relational networks variable was added to the regression analysis. The model was highly significant in predicting crime rates (p < .001). The model explained 50 percent of the total variance in crime rates. Again, the disorder/secondary relational networks variable had a strong and positive direct effect on crime rates (beta = .37, p < .001).

The addition of disorder/secondary relational networks changed the relationship between percent African American and crime rates. Percent African American has an effect on crime rates of .22, of which .14 (64 percent) is transmitted through disorder/secondary relational networks.

The direct effect of percent African American is .08 (36 percent of the total effect).

In both regression models, residential stability has a strong effect on crime rates that is unmediated by disorder/secondary relational networks. Socioeconomic status also is strongly related to crime rates, but disorder/secondary relational networks does account for 39 percent of the variance in that relationship. Percent African American is not as strongly predictive of crime rates as the other structural variables and disorder/secondary relationships explains much of this relationship (64 percent).

MODEL 2: EXPLAINING FEAR OF CRIME

Like crime rates, the index of fear of crime is a metric level variable. Thus, the appropriate technique for examining the effects of the independent variables on the dependent variables was Ordinary Least Squares (OLS) regression. Hierarchical Linear Analysis (HLM) was also conducted to better assess the contextual effects of neighborhood variables on fear of crime, since the measurement of the dependent variable (fear of crime) justified the use of HLM. One goal of addressing the same question with two statistical techniques was to determine whether use of the increasingly popular statistical approach, HLM, makes a difference in the results.

First, correlations among the independent variables will be examined. Second, the regression results are discussed. Finally, the HLM results are discussed and compared to the OLS regression results.

Bivariate Analysis

Bivariate patterns of association were examined prior to the multivariate analysis. Table 22 displays a matrix of

Table 22: Correlation Matrix of Variables- Fear of Crime Model

	Stability	African American	SES	Disorder	Primary	Secondary	Parochial & Public
African American	.06						
SES	.28*	.40**					
Disorder	.04	.29**	.59**				
Primary	.47**	-.35**	-.03	-.15			
Secondary	.08	-.59**	-.44**	-.58**	.44**		
Parochial & Public	-.14	-.27**	-.41**	.99**	.03	.46**	
Fear of Crime	.08	.63**	.48**	.59**	-.36**	-.49**	-.42**

* = p < .05; ** p < .01

Pearson product-moment correlation coefficients for the variables in the research model predicting fear of crime.

Among the independent variables, residential stability was not significantly correlated with fear of crime (r = .08). Percent African American was the strongest correlate of fear of crime (r = .63, p < .01) and the association was in the expected direction. The higher the percentage of African Americans in a neighborhood, the higher the fear of crime. The correlation between socioeconomic status and fear of crime was also strong and in the expected direction (r = .48, p < .01).

All of the intervening variables had significant bivariate correlations with fear of crime and all were in the expected direction. Disorder was the variable most strongly correlated with fear of crime among the intervening variables (r = .59, p < .01). The higher the level of perceived disorder in a neighborhood, the higher the fear of crime. The second highest bivariate correlation was between fear of crime and secondary relational networks (r = -.49, p < .01). The more that neighbors trust and interact with each other the lower their fear of crime. Parochial/public control was also significantly correlated with fear of crime (r = -.42, p < .001). The more that neighbors are willing to intervene in neighborhood disturbances, the lower the fear of crime. Finally, primary relational networks was significantlycorrelated with fear of crime (r = -.36, p < .001). The more family and friendship networks reported by survey respondents, the lower the fear of crime.

The same multicollinearity problems encountered with the crime rates models exist with the fear of crime analysis. The same high zero-order correlations can be identified, and will be addressed prior to the multivariate analysis.

Problem of Multicollinearity

Bursik and Grasmick make the same predictions regarding fear of crime as they did with crime rates. They predict that the structural variables socioeconomic status, residential stability, and racial heterogeneity predict fear of crime through disorder, primary and secondary relational networks, and parochial/public control.

The estimation of the total, direct, and indirect effects of individual variables in the full theoretically-derived model was impractical due to high multicollinearity. Thus, separate regression models for socioeconomic status and percent African American were conducted. There were several relatively high intercorrelations among the intervening variables disorder, primary and secondary relationships, and parochial/public control. While these high correlations could cause multicollinearity problems, it was impractical to simply drop them from the model, since all are significantly correlated with the dependent variable. All of the intervening variables were therefore included in the regression analysis for fear of crime, but they will be interpreted as a "block effect". That is, no attempt will be made to interpret their unique contribution to the explanation of fear of crime, since collinearity would make individual data values suspect.

Before regression analysis was conducted, the dependent variable fear of crime was tested for normality by examining a histogram and a normal probability plot. The variable was found to be only slightly negatively skewed (Skewness = -.02). Thus it was not transformed.

Regression Analysis

Table 23 presents the OLS regression results with the revised model of fear of crime, using the neighborhood-level structural variables residential stability and socioeconomic status. Percent African American was excluded from the first run. The regression model was estimated using confirmatory specification in the total effects model. Thus, the structural variables were entered into the analysis first.

The total effects model was significant in predicting fear of crime (R^2 = .22, p< .001). This model explained 22 percent of the variance in fear of crime. Socioeconomic status significantly predicted fear of crime (beta = .48, p < .001). The lower the socioeconomic status in a neighborhood the higher the fear of crime. Residential stability did not have a significant total effect on fear of crime.

In the direct effects model, disorder, primary and secondary relational networks, and parochial/public control were added as a block of variables representing individual-level variables. Addition of the four aggregated individual-level variables increased the variance explained from 22 percent to 49 percent (p < .001).

The second column in Table 23 reports the indirect effect of SES on fear of crime, through the individual-level variables. Recall that this is estimated by subtracting the direct effects of the independent variables from their total effects (Alwin and Hauser, 1975).

The regression coefficient for SES in the total effects model was .48 (p < .001). In the indirect effect model, the regression coefficient was .12. Thus, of the total effect of SES on fear of crime (.48), 75 percent (.48-.12/.48) is mediated by the intervening variables, and .12 (25 percent) of the total effect (.48) is unmediated or a direct effect.

Table 23: Total, Direct, and Indirect Effects of Residential Stability and SES on Fear of Crime with Disorder, Primary & Secondary Relationships, & Parochial/Public Control Intervening

Independent Variables	Standardized Regression Coefficients		
	Total Effect	Indirect Effect	Direct Effect
Residential Stability	.06	.13	.19
SES	.48***	.36	.12
Disorder			.39**
Primary Relational Networks			-.37**
Secondary Relational Networks			-.02
Parochial/Public Control			-.10
R-Square	.22***		.49***

**p < .01; ***p < .001

Table 24 presents the results of OLS regression on fear of crime using the same concepts as the previous model except that percent African American replaces socioeconomic status in the model. The structural variables were entered into the analysis first. The total effects model was significant in predicting fear of crime ($R2 = .40$, p < .001). This model explained 40 percent of the variance in fear of crime.

Table 24: Total, Direct, and Indirect Effects of Residential Stability and Percent African American on Fear of Crime with Disorder, Primary & Secondary Relationships, & Parochial/Public Control Intervening

Independent Variables	Standardized Regression Coefficients		
	Total Effect	Indirect Effect	Direct Effect
Residential Stability	.06	.13	.19
Percent African American	.63***	.13	.50***
Disorder			.49***
Primary Relational Networks			-.27*
Secondary Relational Networks			.23
Parochial/Public Control			-.08
R-Square	.40***		.63***

*p < .05; ***p < .001

Examination of the standardized regression coefficients indicates that percent African American significantly predicted fear of crime (beta = .63, p < .001). Residential stability did not have a significant total effect on fear of crime.

In the direct effects model, disorder, primary and secondary relational networks, and parochial/public control were again added as a block of variables representing the individual-level variables. Addition of the four aggregated individual-level variables increased the variance explained from 40 percent to 63 percent (p < .001).

The second column of Table 24 reports the indirect effect of percent African American on fear of crime, through the individual-level variables. The regression coefficients for percent African American in the total effects model was .63 (p<.001). In the direct effect model, the regression coefficient was beta .50 (p<.001). Thus, of the total effect of percent African American on fear of crime (.63), 20 percent (.63-.50/.63) is mediated by the intervening variables and .50 (80 percent) of the total effect is unmediated or a direct effect.

In both regression models residential stability did not significantly predict fear of crime. Socioeconomic status had a strong effect on fear of crime and the intervening variables explained 75 percent of the variance in that relationship. Percent African American had a strong effect on fear of crime. The intervening variables accounted for 20 percent of the variance in that relationship.

HLM Analysis

Introduction
Bursik and Grasmick's theory predicts how neighborhoods affect individuals within them and these predictions can be formulated as two-level hierarchical linear models. A hierarchy consists of lower-level observations (individual-level data) nested within higher levels (e.g., aggregated-level data). Examples include individual students nested within schools, individual employees nested within organizations, and in this case, individuals nested within neighborhoods (Kreft and Leeuw, 1998).

Historically, multilevel problems have led to analysis approaches that move all variables by aggregation or disaggregation to one single level of interest, followed by multiple regression or some other common statistical analysis (Hox, 1995). This in fact, was the procedure used to this point in the present research.

Analyzing variables from different levels at one single common level creates some problems. The first set of problems are statistical. If the individual-level data are aggregated (as in the previous OLS regression analyses), the result is that different data values from many subunits are combined into fewer values for fewer higher level units. Information is lost, and the statistical analysis loses power.

On the other hand, if the aggregated-level data are disaggregated, the result is that a few data values from a small number of large units are separated into values for a much larger number of subunits. Ordinary statistical tests treat all of these disaggregated data values as independent information from this artificially much larger sample. The proper sample size for these variables is the number of higher level units. Using the higher number of disaggregated cases for the sample size leads to significance tests that reject the null-hypothesis far more often than the nominal alpha level suggests (Hox, 1995).

The other problems are conceptual. If the analyst is not careful in the interpretation of results, s/he may commit the ecological fallacy, which consists of analyzing the data at one level, and drawing conclusions at another level. The ecological fallacy is interpreting aggregated data at the individual level. Drawing inferences at a higher level from analyses performed at a lower level is just as misleading and is called the atomistic fallacy (Hox, 1995).

Multilevel Regression Models
The solution to these problem is suggested in the use of multilevel or hierarchical regression models. The full multilevel regression model assumes that there is a hierarchical data set, with one single dependent variable that is measured at the lowest individual-level and explanatory variables at all existing levels. Conceptually,

the model can be viewed as a hierarchical system of regression equations. With multilevel models, one can set up a separate regression equation in each separate neighborhood to predict the dependent variable Y by the explanatory variable X as follows:

$$Y_{ij} = \beta_{oj} + \beta_{ij} X_{ij} + e_{ij} \qquad \text{[Equation 1]}$$

In this regression equation β_{oj} is the usual intercept, β_{ij} is the usual regression coefficient (regression slope), and e_{ij} is the usual residual error term. The subscript j is for the neighborhoods and the subscript i is for the individuals within the neighborhoods. In the usual regression model we assume that each neighborhood is characterized by a different intercept coefficient β_{oj} and also a different slope coefficient β_{ij} (Hox, 1995).

In other words, the intercept and slope coefficients are assumed to vary across neighborhoods; for this reason they are often referred to as random coefficients. Each neighborhood is characterized by its own specific value for the intercept and the slope coefficient for each individual-level variable.

Across all neighborhoods, the regression coefficients β_j have a distribution with some mean and variance. The next step in the hierarchical regression model is to predict the variation of the regression coefficients β_j by introducing explanatory variables at the neighborhood level, as follows:

$$\beta_{0j} = \Upsilon_{00} + \Upsilon_{01} Z_j + u_{0j}, \qquad \text{[Equation 2]}$$
and
$$\beta_{1j} = \Upsilon_{10} + \Upsilon_{11} Z_j + u_{1j}. \qquad \text{[Equation 3]}$$

The u-terms u_{0j} and u_{1j} in the above equations are random or residual error terms at the neighborhood level. The residual errors u_j are assumed to have a mean of zero, and to be independent from the residual errors e_{ij} at the individual-level. The variance of the residual errors u_{0j} is specified as σ_{00}, and the variance of the residual errors u_{1j} is specified as σ_{11}. The covariance σ_{11} between the residual error terms u_{0j} and u_{1j} is not assumed to be zero (Hox, 1995).

In the equations above Υ represents regression coefficients. They are not assumed to vary across neighborhoods and thus have no subscript j to indicate which neighborhood they belong to.

They apply to all neighborhoods. Therefore they are referred to as fixed coefficients. All between neighborhood variation left in the β coefficients after predicting these with the neighborhood variable Z_j is assumed to be residual error variation, which is captured by the residual error terms u_j (Hox, 1995).

The above equations can be written as one single regression equation by substituting equations 2 and 3 into equation 1.

$$Y_{ij} = \Upsilon_{00} + \Upsilon_{10} X_{ij} + \Upsilon_{11} Z_j X_{ij} + u_{1j} X_{ij} + u_{0j} + e_{ij} \quad \text{[Equation 4]}$$

The segment $\Upsilon_{00} + \Upsilon_{10} X_{ij} + \Upsilon_{11} Z_j X_{ij}$ in the equation above contains all the fixed coefficients; for this reason this is often called the fixed part of the model. The segment $u_{1j} X_{ij} + u_{0j} + e_{ij}$ in the above equation contains all the random error terms; for this reason this is often called the random part of the model. The term $Z_j X_{ij}$ is an interaction term that appears in the model as a consequence of modeling the varying regression slope β_{1j} of the individual-level variable X_{ij} with the neighborhood-level variable Z_j. This moderator effect of Z on the relationship between the dependent variable Y and X is expressed as a cross-level interaction (Hox, 1995).

Part of the argument for the need of multilevel models with grouped data is because the observations in the same group are generally more similar than the observations from different groups, which violates the assumption of independence of all observations. This lack of independence can be expressed as a correlation coefficient called the intra-class correlation (ρ). The intra-class correlation is estimated in multilevel models by not including any explanatory variables at either level. This is called an intercept-only or unconditional model. The intra class correlation is estimated from the following equation:

$$\rho = \sigma_{00} / (\sigma_{00} + \sigma^2).$$

Unconditional Model

The first model utilized in the HLM analysis is termed an unconditional model. It is simply a one-way ANOVA with random effects. It provides useful information about how much variation in fear of crime lies within and between neighborhoods and is used as a comparison model for the variance statistics in subsequent models. Table 25 presents the results.

The table lists the variance components. The individual-level variance is $\sigma^2 = 6.28$. The neighborhood-level variance is $\sigma_{00} = .93$, $\chi^2 = 303.97$, p <.001). Thus, there is significant variation among neighborhoods in levels of fear of crime. Using the variance components we can calculate the intra-class correlation or the proportion of variance between neighborhoods.

$$\rho = \sigma_{00}/(\sigma_{00} + \sigma^2) = .93/(.93 + 6.28) = .13$$

This indicates that about 13 percent of the variance in fear of crime is between neighborhoods. These estimates indicate that most of the variation in fear of crime (87 percent) is at the individual level. These results will take on added importance when the independent variables are added to the analysis.

Table 25: Results from Unconditional Model of Fear of Crime

Fixed Effect	Coefficient	
Average neighborhood mean, Υ_{00}	6.91***	
Random Effect	**Variance Component**	χ^2
Neighborhood mean, u_{0j} (σ_{00})	.93***	303.97
Level-1 effect, e_{ij} (σ^2)	6.28	
ρ	.13	

***p < .001

Regression with Means-as-Outcomes for Stability and SES

With the regression as outcomes model, the individual-level model remains the same as in the unconditional model. That is, the individual-level variables disorder, primary relational networks, secondary relational networks, and parochial/public control are not added to the analysis at this point. Fear of crime is viewed as varying around its neighborhood mean. The neighborhood-level model is elaborated now so that each neighborhood's mean level of fear of crime is predicted by residential stability, socioeconomic status, and percent African American.

Since HLM analysis shares the same assumptions as OLS regression, the multicollinearity that was problematic in interpreting the results in the regression analysis remains a problem in interpreting HLM. Therefore, the HLM analysis will be conducted with SES and percent African American added separately to the model.

Recall that the multicollinearity that occurred previously among the individual-level variables were aggregated measures. That is, in the regression analysis, measures from 1622 individual surveys were aggregated to the neighborhood-level of measurement resulting in sixty-six neighborhoods or cases. In the HLM analysis, all 1622 cases are used at the individual-level of measurement.

Table 26 displays the bivariate correlations at the individual-level of measurement. As might be expected, the bivariate correlations for the individual-level measurements revealed much lower correlations than the aggregated measures. The highest correlation was -.29. Thus, multicollinearity among the intervening variables is not a problem in this analysis allowing for interpretation of each individual-level variable.

$$\beta_{0j} = \Upsilon_{00} + \Upsilon_{01}(\text{Stability})_j + \Upsilon_{02}(\text{SES})_j + u_{0j},$$

Where Υ_{00} is the intercept, Υ_{01} is the effect of stability on b_{0j} (fear of crime), and Υ_{02} is the effect of SES on b_{0j}. Whereas the random variable u_{0j} had been the deviation of neighborhood j's mean from the grand mean in the unconditional model, it now represents the residual variance.

Table 27 provides estimates and hypothesis tests for the fixed effects and the variances of the random effects. The results indicate that socioeconomic status had a significant effect on fear of crime ($\Upsilon_{02} = .20$, p < .001). Residential stability was not a significant predictor of fear of crime.

Table 27 also displays the residual variance between neighborhoods $\sigma_{00} = .67$, which is smaller than the original $\sigma_{00} = .93$ estimated in the unconditional model and presented in table 26.

Table 26: Correlation Matrix of Individual-Level Variables Fear of Crime Model

	Disorder	Primary Relation-ships	Secondary Relation-ships	Paro-chial & Public
Primary	.01			
Secondary	-.05	.23**		
Parochial & Public	-.29**	.02	.14**	
Fear of Crime	.38**	-.11**	-.09**	-.17**

** $p < .01$

Table 27: Results from Means as Outcomes Model of Fear of Crime for Stability and SES

Fixed Effect	Coefficient		
Model for neighborhood means			
Intercept, Υ_{00}	6.91***		
Stability[a], Υ_{01}	-.06		
SES[a], Υ_{02}	.20***		
Random Effect	**Variance Component**	χ^2	**Reduction in Variance**
Neighborhood mean, u_{0j} (σ_{00})	.67***	164.99	28%
Level-1 effect	6.28		
ρ	.10		

*** $p < .001$

a: The unstandardized coefficients were standardized from the following formula: Standard coefficient = (unstandardized coefficient) x (standard deviation of explanatory variable)/Standard Deviation of Dependent Variable (Hox, 1995; p. 24).

By comparing the σ_{00} estimates across the two models, we can develop an index of the proportion of reduction in neighborhood-level variance or the variance explained by adding stability and SES to the analysis.

Proportion variance explained in β_{0j} = σ_{00}(unconditional model) – σ_{00} (stability and SES) ÷ σ_{00}(unconditional model)

Using the above equation, adding stability and SES reduced the between neighborhood variance by (.93-.67)/.93 = .28 or 28 percent. The estimated proportion of variance between neighborhoods explained by the model with stability and SES is 28 percent. That is, 28 percent of the between-neighborhood variance in fear of crime is accounted for by stability and SES.

After removing the effect of the independent variables, the intra-class correlation (ρ) which had been 13 percent, is now reduced to 10 percent:

$$\rho = \sigma_{00}/(\sigma_{00} + \sigma^2)$$

$$\rho = .67/(.67 + 6.28) = .10$$

The estimated ρ is now a conditional intra-class correlation and measures degree of dependence among observations within neighborhoods that are of the same residential stability and socioeconomic status. It is an indication of the degree to which individuals share common experiences; in other words group homogeneity. If the intra-class correlation is high, neighborhoods are very different from each other with respect to residential stability and SES. If the intra-class correlation is low, neighborhoods are only slightly different from each other.

Do fear of crime levels vary significantly once residential stability and SES are controlled? Here the null hypothesis that $\sigma_{00} = 0$, where σ_{00} is now a residual variance, is tested by means of a Chi-Square Statistic. In this case, the χ^2 statistic has a value of 239.18 (p < .001), indicating that the null hypothesis is easily rejected. After controlling for the independent variables, significant variation among neighborhood fear of crime remains to be explained.

Regression with Means-as-Outcomes for Stability and Percent African American

The neighborhood-level model is estimated now so that each neighborhood's mean level of fear of crime is predicted by residential stability and percent African American.

$\beta_{0j} = \Upsilon_{00} + \Upsilon_{01}(Stability)_j + \Upsilon_{02}(Percent\ African\ American)_j + u_{0j},$

Where Υ_{00} is the intercept, Υ_{01} is the effect of stability on b_{0j}(fear of crime), and Υ_{02} is the effect of percent African American on b_{0j}.

Table 28 provides estimates and hypothesis tests for the fixed effects and the variances of the random effects. The results indicate that the racial composition of neighborhoods has a significant positive effect on fear of crime ($\Upsilon_{02} = .26$, p < .001). Again, residential stability was not a significant predictor of fear of crime. The residual variance between neighborhoods, $\sigma_{00} = .44$, is smaller than the original $\sigma_{00} = .93$ estimated in the unconditional model and is presented in table 28.

Table 28: Results from Means as Outcomes Model of Fear of Crime for Stability and Percent African American

Fixed Effect	Coefficient		
Model for neighborhood means			
Intercept, Υ_{00}	6.90***		
Stability[a], Υ_{01}	.02		
African American, Υ_{02}	.26***		
Random Effect	**Variance Component**	χ^2	**Reduction in Variance**
Neighborhood mean, u_{0j} (σ_{00})	.44***	178.91	53%
Level-1 effect	6.28		
ρ	.07		

*** p <.001

By comparing the σ_{00} estimates across the two models, again we can develop an index of the proportion reduction in variance or, loosely speaking, the variance explained by the level-2 predictor variables. The estimated proportion of reduction in variance between neighborhoods with the independent variables stability and SES included in the model is $(.93-.44)/.93 = .53$ or 53 percent. Thus, 53 percent of the between-neighborhood variance in fear of crime is accounted for by stability and percent African American.

After removing the effect of the independent variables, the intra-class correlation which had been 13 percent in the unconditional model, is now reduced to 7 percent:

$$\rho = \tau_{00}/(\tau_{00} + \sigma^2)$$
$$= .44/(.44 + 6.28) = .07$$

Neighborhoods are only slightly different from each other with respect to residential stability and percent African American in mean perceptions of fear of crime. Do fear of crime levels vary significantly once residential stability and percent African American are controlled? Here the null hypothesis that $\sigma_{00} = 0$, where σ_{00} is now a residual variance, is tested by means of a Chi-Square Statistic. In this case, the χ^2 statistic has a value of 178.91 ($p < .001$), indicating that the null hypothesis is easily rejected. After controlling for the independent variables, significant variation among neighborhood fear of crime remains to be explained.

Full HLM Model for Fear of Crime with Stability and SES

The full explanatory HLM models will now be assessed. Thus, we can begin to understand why some neighborhoods have higher levels of fear of crime than others and why in some neighborhoods the association between disorder and primary relationships and fear of crime is stronger than others. Again, two different HLM models will be estimated with SES and percent African American population.

The full HLM model is termed an intercept and slopes-as-outcomes model and is simply a combination of the neighborhood-level and individual-level models. This analysis can address the following:

1. Does residential stability and SES significantly predict the intercept? For example, γ_{02} will be an indication of whether high SES neighborhoods differ from low SES neighborhoods in mean levels of fear of crime controlling for residential stability.

2. Does stability and SES significantly predict the within-neighborhood slopes? γ_{12} gives us an estimate of whether high SES neighborhoods differ from low SES neighborhoods in terms of the strength of association between individual-level perceptions of disorder and fear of crime.

3. How much variation in the intercepts and the slopes is explained by using stability and SES.

4. After taking into account stability and SES, what is the correlation between the unique neighborhood contributions to the intercept and the slope respectively?

Table 29 displays the results of the full HLM analysis on fear of crime for residential stability and SES. First of all there is significant variation in fear of crime among the sampled neighborhoods ($\gamma_{00} = 6.87$, p < .001). Of the contextual variables, neither residential stability nor SES had a significant effect on fear of crime. Thus, from Table 27 of the total effect of SES on fear of crime (.20), 65 percent (.20-.07/.20) was mediated by disorder, primary and secondary relational networks, and parochial/public control. Thus, .07 (35 percent) is unmediated or a direct effect.

The analysis indicates that among the individual-level variables, disorder was the strongest predictor of fear of crime ($\gamma_{10} = .33$, p < .001). Primary relational networks also had a significant negative effect on fear of crime ($\gamma_{20} = -.09$, p < .001). None of the other individual-level variables had a significant effect on fear of crime.

Table 29 also presents estimates and test statistics for residual variances of the intercepts and slopes. The estimated variances of the disorder-fear of crime slope (u_{1j}), primary relational networks-fear of crime slope (u_{2j}), secondary relational networks-fear of crime slope (u_{3j}), and parochial/public control-fear of crime slope (u_{4j}) are weak

Table 29: Results from the HLM Model of Fear of Crime for Stability and SES

Fixed Effect	Coefficient		
Model for neighborhood means			
Intercept, Υ_{00}	6.87***		
Stability[a], Υ_{01}	.01		
SES, Υ_{02}	.07		
Model for Disorder Slopes			
Intercept, Υ_{10}	.33***		
Stability, Υ_{11}	.01		
SES, Υ_{12}	.00		
Model for Primary Relational Networks Slopes			
Intercept, Υ_{20}	-.09***		
Stability, Υ_{21}	.00		
SES, Υ_{22}	.00		
Model for Secondary Relational Networks Slopes			
Intercept, Υ_{30}	-.03		
Stability, Υ_{31}	.00		
SES, Υ_{32}	-.03		
Model for Parochial/Public Control Slopes			
Intercept, Υ_{40}	-.04		
Stability, Υ_{41}	.01		
SES, Υ_{42}	-.02		
Random Effect	**Variance**	χ^2	**Reduction in Variance**
Neighborhood mean, u_{0j} $(\sigma_{00)}$	.70***	146.73	25%
Level-1 effect	5.33		15%
ρ	.12		

*** p <.001

and not significant. Thus, we can infer that the relationships between these individual-level variables and fear of crime within neighborhoods does not vary significantly across the population of neighborhoods.

There is a small reduction in variance of the neighborhood means once the neighborhood-level variables are controlled. Specifically, whereas the unconditional variance of the intercepts had been $\sigma_{00} = .93$ in the unconditional model (See Table 25), the residual variance is now $\sigma_{00} = .70$. Thus, adding residential stability and SES as a predictor of fear of crime reduced the between-neighborhood variance by 25 percent. Hence we can conclude that stability and SES accounts for about 25 percent of the neighborhood-level variance in fear of crime.

We can also develop an index of the proportion of reduction in variance or variance explained at the individual-level by comparing σ^2 estimates from the unconditional model to the full HLM model. Whereas the unconditional individual-level variance was $\sigma^2 = 6.28$, the residual variance is now $\sigma^2 = 5.33$. Adding stability and SES reduced the within-neighborhood variance by 15 percent. Thus, 15 percent of the within neighborhood variance in fear of crime is accounted for by the individual-level variables.

After removing the effect of the neighborhood-level and individual-level variables, the intra-class correlation which had been 13 percent in the unconditional model, is now reduced to only 12 percent:

$$\rho = \sigma_{00}/(\sigma_{00} + \sigma^2)$$
$$= .70/(.70 + 5.33) = .12$$

A test of the null hypothesis that no residual variance remains to be explained is rejected (χ^2 statistic is 146.73, df 63, p < .001). Thus, the results encourage a search for further neighborhood-level variables that might help account for the remaining variation in fear of crime.

Full HLM Model for Fear of Crime with Stability and Percent African-American

Another intercepts and slopes-as-outcomes model was estimated with residential stability and percent African American as the neighborhood-level predictor variables with the same individual-level intervening variables. Table 30 displays the results of the full HLM analysis on fear of crime for residential stability and percent African American.

First of all there is significant variation in fear of crime among the sampled neighborhoods ($\Upsilon_{00} = 6.88$, p < .001). Again, residential stability did not have a significant effect on fear of crime. Percent African American had a significant positive effect on fear of crime ($\Upsilon_{02} = .19$, p < .001).

From Table 28, of the total effect of percent African American on fear of crime (.26), 27 percent (.26-.19/.26) was mediated by the individual-level variables, and .19 (73 percent) is unmediated or a direct effect.

Among the individual-level variables, disorder was the better predictor of fear of crime again ($\Upsilon_{10} = .34$, p < .001). Primary relational networks also had a significant negative effect on fear of crime ($\Upsilon_{20} = -.09$, p < .001). Again, none of the other individual-level variables significantly predicted fear of crime.

There was also a significant cross-level or interaction effect between percent African American and disorder ($\Upsilon_{12} = -.01$, p < .05). There is a tendency that the higher the racial diversity of the neighborhood the higher the mean levels of perceptions of disorder by neighborhood residents.

Table 30 presents estimates and test statistics for residual variances of the intercepts and slopes. The estimated variances of the disorder-fear of crime slope (u_{1j}), primary relational networks-fear of crime slope (u_{2j}),

Table 30: Full HLM of Fear of Crime for Stability and Percent African American

Fixed Effect	Coefficient		
Model for neighborhood means			
Intercept, Υ_{00}	6.88***		
Stability[a], Υ_{01}	.04		
African American, Υ_{02}	.19***		
Model for Disorder Slopes			
Intercept, Υ_{10}	.34***		
Stability, Υ_{11}	.01		
African American, Υ_{12}	.01*		
Model for Primary Relational Networks Slopes			
Intercept, Υ_{20}	-.09***		
Stability, Υ_{21}	.00		
African American, Υ_{22}	-.01		
Model for Secondary Relational Networks Slopes			
Intercept, Υ_{30}	-.02		
Stability, Υ_{31}	-.01		
African American, Υ_{32}	-.02		
Model for Parochial/Public Control Slopes			
Intercept, Υ_{40}	-.04		
Stability, Υ_{41}	.01		
African American, Υ_{42}	-.03		
Random Effect	**Variance**	χ^2	**Variance Reduction**
Neighborhood mean, u_{0j} (σ_{00})	.23***	105.14	75%
Level-1 effect	5.33		15%
ρ	.12		

* < .05; *** p < .001

secondary relational networks-fear of crime slope (u_{3j}), and parochial/public control-fear of crime slope (u_{4j}) are weak and not significant. Thus, we can infer that the relationships between these individual-level variables and fear of crime within neighborhoods does not vary significantly across the population of neighborhoods.

There is a reduction in variance of the neighborhood means once the neighborhood-level variables are controlled. Specifically, whereas the unconditional variance of the intercepts had been $\sigma_{00} = .93$ in the unconditional model (see Table 25), the residual variance is now $\sigma_{00} = .23$. Thus, adding residential stability and percent African American as a predictor of fear of crime reduced the between-neighborhood variance by 75 percent. Thus, 75 percent of the within neighborhood variance in fear of crime is accounted for by stability and percent African American.

Again an index of the proportion of reduction in variance or variance explained is developed at the individual-level by comparing σ^2 estimates from the unconditional model to the full HLM model. Whereas the unconditional individual-level variance was $\sigma^2 = 6.28$, the residual variance is now $\sigma^2 = 5.33$. Adding stability and percent African American reduced the within-neighborhood variance by 15 percent. This is the exact same results as the stability and SES model indicating that 15 percent of the within-neighborhood variance in fear of crime is accounted for the by the individual-level variables.

After removing the effect of the neighborhood-level and individual-level variables, the intra-class correlation which had been 13 percent in the unconditional model, is now reduced to only 4 percent:

$$\rho = \sigma_{00}/(\sigma_{00} + \sigma^2)$$
$$= .23/(.23 + 5.33) = .04$$

A test of the null hypothesis that no residual variance remains to be explained is rejected (χ^2 statistic is 105.14, df 63, p < .001). Thus, the results encourage a search for further neighborhood-level variables that might help account for the remaining variation in fear of crime.

A comparison of the regression and HLM models reveals similar results overall for the neighborhood-level variables. In both the OLS Regression and HLM analyses, neighborhood residential stability was not a significant predictor of fear of crime. In both analyses neighborhood socioeconomic status had a significant effect on fear of crime that was mediated by the individual-level variables. Finally, in both analyses racial concentration had a positive and significant effect on fear of crime that was only moderately mediated by the individual-level variables.

In the regression analysis multicollinearity among the aggregated individual-level variables prevented examination of their direct effects on fear of crime. Because there was not substantial multicollinearity among the non-aggregated individual-level variables, HLM analysis allowed for an examination of the direct effect of each variable. Another value of HLM was that because this technique uses all available data (66 neighborhoods and 1622 surveys nested within these neighborhoods), it is quite likely that the regression coefficients are more realistic. Finally, HLM allows for a decomposition of variance explained between and within neighborhoods for the dependent variable.

The final chapter of this dissertation will discuss the implications of the analysis for Bursik and Grasmick's systemic neighborhood control theory, measurement and statistical analysis, and policy implications of the analysis. The final chapter will also include conclusions from this study.

CHAPTER 7

SUMMARY AND DISCUSSION

INTRODUCTION

The primary purpose of this study was to conduct a test of Bursik and Grasmick's systemic neighborhood control theory. Research models were estimated to explain neighborhood crime rates and fear of crime. Ordinary Least Squares Regression was used to explain crime rates and fear of crime where neighborhood is the unit of analysis. Because of the hierarchical structure of the data (individuals surveyed within neighborhoods), Hierarchical Linear Modeling (HLM) was also used to explain fear of crime.

This chapter briefly summarizes the findings from the analyses and suggests their implications for Bursik and Grasmick's theory and for policy. Limitations of the present research are discussed and suggestions are made for further research.

SUMMARY AND DISCUSSION OF FINDINGS

Explaining Crime Rates

Bursik and Grasmick predicted that the social structure of neighborhoods, based on population instability, socioeconomic status, and racial heterogeneity, affects the rate of crime because of an inability of neighborhoods to maintain social control. Low socioeconomic status neighborhoods with their rapid population change and greater racial heterogeneity are more likely to have breakdowns in family and friendship networks. A lack of interaction with family and friends results in a loss of neighborhood social control, thereby increasing the crime rates.

This research lends partial support to Bursik and Grasmick's propositions. Neighborhood disorder and secondary relationships accounted for fully 64 percent of the effect of the percentage of neighborhoods that are African American on crime rates. In other words, predominantly minority neighborhoods in this sample, which are also lower level socioeconomic status neighborhoods, tend to have high levels of physical and social disorder and low levels of neighborhood interaction and mutual trust, and this results in higher rates of crime. Physical disorder includes vandalism, vacant housing, poor upkeep of property, litter in the streets, vacant lots with trash. Social disorder includes bad elements moving in, fighting and arguing, and unsupervised youth. This finding lends support to Bursik and Grasmick's contention that when disorder becomes highly visible in a community, residents may feel demoralized, helpless, and angry at being crowded out of community life, resulting in deviant behavior.

The results coincide with Lewis and Salem's (1986) findings that high levels of disorder in poor urban neighborhoods tend to be associated with lower rates of mutual helping behavior among residents in the area. In highly disorderly neighborhoods, mutual distrust and hostility are rampant, and antipathy between newcomers and long-term residents prevails. Residents of urban minority areas tend to view each other with suspicion (Taub, Taylor, and Dunham, 1981; Greenberg et al., 1982). Without such support, people feel powerless, impotent, and vulnerable in the face of crime (Skogan, 1990). Also, perceptions of disorder appear to undermine the belief that problems can be solved locally; they increase the sense of personal isolation, and spread the perception that no one will come to their aid when in trouble (Lewis and Salem, 1986).

Bursik and Grasmick predicted that residential instability would have the largest effect of the structural variables on crime rates and that prediction held true in this research. However, the level of physical and social disorder, family and friendship networks, neighborhood interaction and mutual trust, and informal social control did not explain away this relationship. These hypothesized intervening variables were also not very effective in explaining the impact of low socioeconomic status on the rate of crime.

In this regard, Wilson (1987) provides a convincing structural argument concerning the rise of inner-city social problems since the 1950s and 1960s. He claims that inner cities have undergone a tremendous social transformation best captured by the terms "concentration effect" and "social buffer". By concentration effect, he means constraints on access to jobs, availability of marriageable partners, and exposure to conventional role models. Social buffer refers to the presence of a sufficient number of working and middle-class professional families to absorb the shock or cushion the effect of uneven economic growth on inner-city neighborhoods. The removal of working and middle-class neighborhoods has made it more difficult to sustain the basic institutions (churches, schools, industry) in the inner city.

Explaining Fear of Crime

Bursik and Grasmick suggest that the neighborhood characteristics and processes resulting in high rates of crime also result in fear of crime. Thus, the same research models used to explain crime rates were also used to explain fear of crime. The results indicated that the mechanisms in neighborhoods leading to higher crime rates are not exactly the same as those leading to fear of crime.

First of all, residential stability was the strongest predictor of crime rates in the sampled neighborhoods but it was not related to fear of crime. Both the regression and HLM analysis confirm this result. Residential stability has not been modeled in previous fear of crime studies and thus this result cannot be compared to previous research.

Of the structural variables in this research, the percentage of the neighborhood that was African American was the best predictor of fear of crime. This is consistent with the findings of a number of researchers who have found a relationship between racial and ethnic diversity in an area and fear of crime (Moeller, 1989; Ortega and Myles, 1987; and Parker and Ray, 1990).

Bursik and Grasmick believe that racially diverse neighborhoods tend to have social boundaries that limit the breadth of neighborhood interaction. They suggest that these social boundaries increase the levels of fear in neighborhoods due to mutual distrust among groups in the area. This expectation is not supported by this study.

A possible explanation lies in the indirect victimization theory of fear of crime. This theory suggests that groups who perceive themselves as vulnerable to crime will have higher levels of fear. Lewis and Salem (1986) claim that high levels of social interaction may actually heighten fear of crime and not lower it as Bursik and Grasmick predict. According to this line of thought, a high level of social interaction is believed to lead to the learning of victimization of others in the neighborhood thereby heightening fear (Lewis and Salem, 1986).

Socioeconomic status had a significant negative effect on fear of crime. Unlike racial diversity, this effect was substantially mediated by the level of disorder and primary relational networks. In other words, poor urban neighborhoods tend to have high levels of physical disorder (litter, abandoned buildings, trash in vacant lots) and social disorder (noise, loitering teens, and people fighting and arguing) with fewer family and friends around, and this results in higher levels of fear of crime. Disorder was much more important in explaining fear of crime than was the number of family and friends in the neighborhood.

These results are consistent with Skogan's (1990) findings. He found that fear is a frequent response to disorder, especially social disorder. Disorderly people are unpredictable by everyday standards, and some are potentially violent. People that Skogan and associates talked to implied that abandoned buildings may harbor criminals or drug dealers. Corner gangs are often menacing, especially for women and the elderly. Inter-group conflicts such as arguments between family members, landlords and tenants, or racial conflicts send signals for potential violence.

Visible physical decay may also spark fear of crime, because many people have come to associate it with higher levels of risk (Skogan, 1990). Skogan argues that one of the things that differentiates fear of crime from concern about other risks is that people identify the incidence of crime with environmental cues. They called these "the signs of crime," and their presence is taken as an early warning of impending danger.

Limitations of the Research

There are several limitations to this research that deserve mention. First of all, this study utilized secondary data analysis. The disadvantage of using secondary data analysis is that the data were collected for a different purpose. As a result, there were no survey questions concerning effective socialization, which is a concept from the systemic theory that had to be left out. There were also very few questions concerning the public level of control which Bursik and Grasmick felt was an important concept in their theory.

Additionally, sample size was potentially a problem for the OLS regression analysis. There were only sixty-six neighborhoods for the analysis. Also, because of the small sample size a more parsimonious test of the theory was conducted. Other concepts that Bursik and Grasmick suggest are important to their theory such as opportunity and changing ecological structures were not incorporated into the analysis.

Another important limitation of this research is that it is cross-sectional. A longitudinal design measuring change in neighborhood structure, organization, crime rates and fear of crime would have been preferable.

Finally, the use of crime rate data has been criticized in neighborhood-level studies. According to Hagan et al. (1978) and Smith (1986) lower-status communities may have higher rates of crime in part because of greater police concentration in poor urban neighborhoods.

Suggestions for Further Research

Elliott et al. (1996) believe that in many respects the theoretical and empirical discussion of neighborhood crime studies is still at a rudimentary level because most previous research in this area has not adequately explained the mechanisms by which neighborhoods influence crime (and fear of crime). The results from this research suggest that we need to continue the search for those mechanisms.

One possibility is competing neighborhood crime and fear of crime theories. I have already mentioned Wilson's (1987) structural explanation for various social maladies plaguing America's inner cities. Another possibility lies in Sampson's argument. Sampson (1997) believes that differential cultural organization has been overlooked as a possible explanation for inner-city crime. He cites several ethnographic studies that generally support the notion that structurally disorganized communities are conducive to the emergence of age-graded subcultures that foster a tolerance for crime and deviance.

Kornhauser (1978) and Bursik (1988) point to a substantial body of research that has failed to uncover the existence of cultural values that prescribe crime and violence. Sampson (1997) claims that both ethnographic and survey research are compatible as long as we emphasize the situational and contextual basis of value attenuation rather than an autonomous culture that positively values violence at all times and places. That is, even though conventional norms may be pervasive in any neighborhood, it is still the case that tolerance of deviance may vary across structural and situational contexts. There are few neighborhood-level crime studies using survey research that have explored these ideas.

Sampson (1997) also suggests that future neighborhood-level crime studies investigate the effects of structural disadvantage on child development and socialization. He claims that the dominant perspectives on neighborhood-level theories tend to emphasize social structural characteristics thought to influence the motivation in later adolescent and adult crime (e.g., economic deprivation and inequality). Aspects of child development such as prenatal care, cognitive development, abuse/neglect, and the daily supervision of children are usually not considered. He highlights the empirical connection between the health and developmental-related problems of children and rates of adult crime. He also suggests that criminologists and developmental theorists alike tend to view child socialization as an interpersonal activity that takes place in the home without considering that parenting styles may be an adaptation to the social organization of the community.

Another suggestion for further research involves the use of multilevel models. Most previous research on crime involves the study of either individual effects or community-level effects. Almost no research has examined both (Reiss, 1986; Gottfredson and Taylor, 1986). Sampson and Lauritsen (1994) specifically note that multi-level hierarchical modeling is appealing as a statistical technique to address this limitation. Recently software has been developed that combines multilevel modeling and path analysis. This technique would allow for tests of more complex and possibly more meaningful theoretical models.

Policy Implications

Because Bursik and Gramick's theory is a neighborhood control theory, it is important to note that social control (as measured in this dissertation) was not related to neighborhood crime rates or fear of crime. This finding suggests that high poverty, racially segregated, and highly mobile neighborhoods do not organize effectively, and even if they do, it has little effect on crime or fear of crime. Bursik and Grasmick admit that those communities most in need of effective crime control programs often are those characterized by a very segmented set of networks that may be difficult to unite in a collective effort. The same problems confront organized efforts to reduce disorder.

Bursik and Grasmick included disorder as an "extension" to their theory. This research suggests that it should take a more prominent position in neighborhood-crime and fear of crime studies. The question is how do we confront disorder? Physical and social disorder suggest neighborhood crime prevention organizations such Neighborhood Watch, Project ID, or community policing. However, Skogan (1990) states that systematic studies of the distribution of anti-crime organizations across neighborhoods indicate that they are uncommon where they are most needed- in low-income, heterogeneous, deteriorated, unstable, higher-crime areas.

Skogan (1990) evaluated several federally funded pilot programs designed to combat disorder in urban neighborhoods. These programs were well organized and carried out by experienced professionals and yet had little impact on the level of disorder or perceptions of the residents living in these neighborhoods. In some cases the fear of crime actually increased.

Neighborhood organization efforts to effectively deal with disorder have likely faltered for the same reason that Bursik and Grasmick's theory failed to fully account for the impact of social structure on crime and fear of crime. The distribution of disorder mirrors the larger pattern of structured inequality in inner cities. Many features of life in city neighborhoods are shaped in important ways by the political decisions of local governments, banks, real estate developers, housing and transportation policies, and the creation of inner city jobs. These factors call for more fundamental and creative solutions to neighborhood problems than community policing or organizing.

Dreier (1996) states that no other major industrial nation has allowed its cities to face the type of fiscal and social adversity that confront America's urban neighborhoods. The consequences of decades of inattention can be seen by growing poverty, violent crime, homelessness, infant mortality, and widening racial and economic segregation.

Dreier (1996) argues that we are currently caught in a political quagmire where politicians and the public largely believe that government can play no constructive role in eradicating the problems facing urban neighborhoods. Many of today's opinion makers argue that we have tried in the 1960's with the War on Poverty and have failed. To Dreier this argument is unpersuasive because most of these efforts were underfunded, misguided, and sought to serve too many goals. Still, some of these programs that emerged from that period have demonstrated success, despite limited funding and commitment.

Dreier offers three major components to a federal investment strategy to revitalize cities. First, the government must stimulate national economic growth and create jobs with the goal of a full employment economy and focusing major investment in the nation's physical infrastructure within cities. A new public works initiative could help to achieve both goals.

Second, the government must improve the nation's human infrastructure and the productivity of its current and future workforce. Both *Fortune* and *Newsweek* featured articles after the riots in Los Angeles calling for a major national investment in human capital- such as job training, health care, child care, and education to improve the productivity of the workforce ("The Economic Crisis," 1992; "What We Can Do," 1992).

Third, the federal government must invest directly in urban neighborhoods to improve the economic, physical, and social conditions of these communities. Dreier argues that we need to create "place specific" policies that assist residents in upgrading physical, economic, and social conditions that make urban neighborhoods attractive to people with many choices, but without displacing or harming people with few choices.

Place specific policies suggested by Dreier include: providing jobs for neighborhood residents by providing tax breaks for urban investors; creating a vital neighborhood business district with adequate retail services; creating decent affordable housing for residents that promote public safety, so that residents and visitors feel free from crime and disorder; and fostering strong community institutions through which residents participate in improving their own neighborhoods.

CONCLUSION

The primary purpose of this study was to test Bursik and Grasmick's systemic neighborhood control theory. This is an important theory that had not been previously tested. This study provided partial support for it.

Two different statistical techniques were used to test the same theoretical model. While the results were substantively the same, use of OLS regression with aggregated data inflated the intercorrelations of the independent variables making it impossible to interpret their unique contribution to the model. With Hierarchical Linear Modeling, the data remained at their natural level resulting in no significant multicollinearity. This ultimately allowed for an interpretation of the individual-level variables and consequently made this study more interesting.

In conclusion, the research conducted provided partial support for Bursik and Grasmick's theory, but it is clear that further research exploring the mechanisms within neighborhoods that mediate social structure and crime and fear of crime are needed.

Since the 1970s, there has been an increased interest in the role that neighborhoods can play in addressing the problems of disorder, crime, and fear of crime (Rosenbaum, 1986). This results of this study highlights that what happens in neighborhoods may be shaped partly by socioeconomic factors linked to the wider political economy. Strategies to address the social and ecological changes that beset many inner-city neighborhoods need to be considered. Martin Luther King Jr. believed that the politics and distribution of power were inseparable from the possibility of better living conditions for the poor. He wrote in 1967 "When a people are mired in oppression, they realize deliverance only when they have accumulated enough power to enforce change" (King Jr., 1967; p. 26).

References

Akers, Ronald L. 1994. *Criminological Theories: Introduction and Evaluation*. Los Angeles: Roxbury Publishing.Company.

Alwin, Duane F., and Robert M. Hauser. 1979. "The Decomposition of Effects in Path Analysis." *American Sociological Review* *40*:37-47.

Bailey, William C. (1985). "Aggregation and Disaggregation in Cross-Sectional Analyses of Crime Rates: The Case of States, SMSAs and Cities." A Paper Presented to the Annual Meetings of the American Society of Criminology, San Diego.

Beasley, R.W., and G. Antunes. 1974. "The Etiology of Urban Crime: An Ecological Analysis." *Criminology 11*:439-461.

Bennett, Richard R. and Jeanne M. Flavin. 1991. "Determinants of Fear of Crime: The Effect of Cultural Setting." *Justice Quarterly 11*:357-81.

Berry, William D., and Stanley Feldman. 1985. *Multiple Regression in Practice (Quantitative Applications in the Social Sciences, Vol. 50)*. Newbury Park, CA: Sage.

Blalock, Hubert M. 1979. *Intergroup Processes: A Micro-macro Perspective*. New York: Free Press.

Block, R. 1979. "Community, Environment, and Violent Crime." *Criminology 17*:46-57.

Brantingham, P. and Brantingham, P. 1984. *Patterns in Crime*. New York: MacMillian.

Breckinridge, Sophonisba, and Edith Abbott. 1912. *The Delinquent Child and the Home*. New York: Russell Sage Foundation.

Bryk, Anthony S. and Stephen W. Raudenbush. 1992. *Hierarchical Linear Models*: *Applications and Data Analysis Methods.* Newbury Park, CA: Sage.

Burgess, Ernest. 1942. "Introduction." In *Juvenile Delinquency and Urban Areas*, edited by C.R. Shaw and H.D. McKay. Chicago: University of Chicago Press.

Burnstein, L. 1980. "The Analysis of Multilevel Data in Educational Research and Evaluation." *Review of Research in Education 8*: 158-233.

Bursik, Robert J. 1988. "Social Disorganization and Theories of Crime and Delinquency: Problems and Prospects." *Criminology 26*:421-438.

Bursik, Robert J. and Harold G. Grasmick. 1993. *Neighborhoods and Crime: The Dimensions of Effective Community Control.* New York: Lexington Books.

Bursik, Robert J. and J. Webb. 1982. "Community Change and Patterns of Delinquency." *American Journal of Sociology 88*:24-42.

Byrne, J., and Robert J. Sampson. 1986. "Key Issues in the Social Ecology of Crime." In *The Social Ecology of Crime*, edited by J. Byrne and R. J. Sampson. New York: Springer-Verlag.

Carmines, Edward G., and Zeller, Richard A. 1979. *Reliability and Validity Assessment.* Newbury Park, CA: Sage.

Carter, Ronald L., and Kim Q. Hill. 1978. "Criminal's and Noncriminal's Perceptions of Urban Crime." *Criminology 16*:353-371.

Covington, Jeanette and Ralph B. Taylor. 1991. "Fear of Crime in Urban Residential Neighborhoods: Implications of Between- and Within-Neighborhood Sources for Current Models." *The Sociological Quarterly* 32:231-249.

Curry, G. D., and I. Spergel. 1988. "Gang homicide, delinquency, and community." *Criminology 26*:381-406.

Dawley, David. 1992. *A Nation of Lords.* Second Edition. Prospect Heights, IL: Waveland Press.

Dreier, Peter. 1996. "America's Urban Crisis: Symptoms, Causes, and Solutions." In *Race, Poverty, and American Cities*, edited by J. C. Boger and J. W. Wegner. Chapell Hill, NC: North Carolina Press.

Elliott, Delbert S., William J. Wilson, David Huizinga, Robert J. Sampson, Amanda Elliott, and Bruce Rankin. 1996. "The Effects of Neighborhood Disadvantage on Adolescent Development." *Journal of Research in Crime and Delinquency 33*(4):389-426.

Ferraro, Kenneth F., and Randy LaGrange (1987). "The Measurement of Fear of Crime." *Sociological Inquiry 57*:70-101.

Garofalo, James and John Laub. 1978. "The Fear of Crime: Broadening our Perspectives." *Victimiology 3*:242-53.

Gates, L.B. and William .M. Rohe. 1987. "The Measurement of Fear of Crime. " *Urban Affairs Quarterly 22*:425-53.

Glyde, John. 1856. "Locality of Crime in Suffolk." *Journal of the Statistical Society of London 19*: 102-112.

Gottfredson, Stephen D., and Ralph Taylor. 1986. "Person-Environment Interactions in the Prediction of Recidivism." Pp. 133-155 in *The Social Ecology of Crime*, edited by J. W. Byrne and R. J. Sampson. New York: Springer-Verlag.

Gove, W., M. Hughes, and M. Geerken. 1985. "Are Uniform Crime Reports a Valid Indicator of the Index Crimes? An Affirmative Answer with Minor Qualifications." *Criminology 23*: 451-502.

Greenberg, Stephanie W., William M. Rohe, and Jay R. Williams. 1982. *Safe and Secure Neighborhoods: Physical Characteristics and Informal Territorial in High and Low Crime Neighborhoods.* Washington, DC: National Institute of Justice.

Greene, J.R. and Ralph B. Taylor. 1988. "Community-Based Policing and Foot Patrol: Issues of Theory and Evaluation." In J.R. Greene and S.D. Mastrofski (eds.) *Community Policing: Rhetoric or Reality?* (Pp. 195-223), New York: Praeger.

Hair Jr., Joseph F., Rolph E. Anderson, Ronald L. Tatham, and William C. Black. 1995. *Multivariate Data Analysis, 4th Ed.* Englewood Cliffs, NJ: Prentice-Hall.

Hagan, John, A.R. Gillis, and J. Chan. 1978. "Explaining Official Delinquency: A Spatial Study of Class, Conflict, and Control." *Sociological Quarterly 19*: 386-398.

Haghighi, Bahram, and Sorenson, Jon. 1996. "America's Fear of Crime." In T. J. Flanagan and D.R. Longmire (eds.) *Americans View Crime and Justice: A National Public Opinion Survey.* Thousand Oaks, CA: Sage.

Heitgard, J.L., and Robert J. Bursik, Jr. 1987. "Extracommunity Dynamics and the Ecology of Delinquency." *American Journal of Sociology 92*: 775-787.

Hindelang, Michael, Travis Hirschi, and J. Weiss. 1981. *Measuring Delinquency.* Beverly Hills, CA: Sage.

Hope, T. and M. Hough. 1988. "Community Approaches to Reducing Crime." In T. Hope and M. Shaw (eds.) *Communities and Crime Reduction* (Pp. 1-29) London: Her Majesty's Stationary Office.

Horowitz, Ruth. 1983. *Honor and the American Dream.* New Brunswick, NJ: Rutgers University Press.

Hox, J. J. 1995. *Applied Multilevel Modeling.* Amsterdam: TT-Publikaties.

Hunter, Albert J.

1974. *Symbolic Communities.* Chicago. University of Chicago Press.

1985. "Private, Parochial, and Public School Orders: The Problem of Crime and Incivility in Urban Communities." Pp. 23-44 in *The Challenge of Social Control: Citizenship and Institution Building in Modern Society*, edited by Gerald D. Suttles and Mayer N. Zald. Norwood, NJ: Ablex Publishing.

Hunter, Albert J., and Gerald D. Suttles. 1972. "The Expanding Community of Limited Liability." Pp. 44-81 in *The Social Construction of Communities*, by Gerald D. Suttles. Chicago: University of Chicago Press.

Hunter, Albert J. and T.L. Baumer. 1982. "Street Traffic, Social Integration and Fear of Crime." *Sociological Inquiry 52*:122-31.

Kapsis, R. 1976. "Continuities in Delinquency and Riot Patterns in Black Residential Areas." *Social Problems 23*:567-580.

King, Jr., Martin Luther. June 11,1967. "Martin Luther King Defines Black Power." *New York Times*, p. 26.

Kornhauser, Ruth R. 1978. *Social Sources of Delinquency: An Appraisal of Analytic Models.* Chicago: University of Chicago Press.

Kreft, Ita and Jan De Leeuw. *Introducing Multilevel Modeling.* Thousand Oaks, CA: Sage.

Krohn, M. 1986. "The Web of Conformity: A Network Approach to the Explanation of Delinquent Behavior." *Social Problems 33*: 81-93.

Lander, Bernard. 1954. *Toward an Understanding of Juvenile Delinquency.* New York: Columbia University Press.

LaGrange, R.L., and K.F. Ferraro. 1989. "Assessing Age and Gender Differences in Perceived Risk and Fear of Crime." *Criminology 27*: 697-717.

LaGrange, R.L., K.F. Ferraro, and M. Supancic. 1992. "Perceived Risk and Fear of Crime: Role of Social and Physical Incivilities." *Journal of Research in Crime and Delinquency 29*: 311-34.

Lewis, D.A. 1979. "Design Problems in Public Policy Development." *Criminology 17*: 172-83.

Lewis, D.A., and G. Salem. 1986. *Fear of Crime: Incivility and the Production of a Social Problem.* New Brunswick, NJ: Transaction Books.

Liska, Allen E., Andrew Sanchirico, and Mark D. Reed. 1988. "Fear of Crime and Constrained Behavior: Specifying and Estimating a Reciprocal Effects Model." *Social Forces 66*: 827-37.

Lombroso, Cesare. 1911. *Crime: Its Causes and Remedies.* New York: Brown and Company.

Maccoby, E., J. Johnson, and R. Church. 1958. "Community Integration and the Social Control of Juvenile Delinquency." *Journal of Social Issues 14*: 38-51.

Mayhew, Henry 1862. *London Labor and the London Poor.* London: London University Press.

McGarrell, Edmund F., Andrew L. Giacomazzi, and Quint C. Thurman. 1997. "Neighborhood Disorder, Integration, and the Fear of Crime." *Justice Quarterly 14*(3): 479-502.

Merry, S.E. 1981. *Urban Danger.* Philadelphia: Temple University Press.

Messner, S., and K. Tardiff. 1986. "Economic Inequality and Levels of Homicide: An Analysis of Urban Neighborhoods." *Criminology 24*: 297-318.

Mladenka, K., and Kim Q. Hill. 1976. "A Reexamination of the Etiology of Urban Crime." *Criminology 13*: 491-506.

Moeller, G. 1989. "Fear of Criminal Victimization: The Effect of Neighborhood Racial Composition." *Sociological Inquiry 59*: 208-21.

Moore, Joan W. 1978. *Homeboys*. Philadelphia: Temple University Press.

Ortega, Suzanne T. and Jessie L. Myles. 1987. "Race and Gender Effects on Fear of Crime: An Interactive Model with Age." *Criminology 25*: 133-52.

Parker, K.D. and M.C. Ray. 1990. "Fear of Crime: An Assessment of Related Factors." *Sociological Spectrum 10*: 29-40.

Pfohl, Stephen J. 1985. *Images of Deviance and Social Control*. New York: McGraw-Hill.

Reiss Jr., Albert J. 1986. "Why are Communities Important in Understanding Crime?" Pp. 1-33 in A.J. Reiss, Jr., and M. Tonry, eds., *Communities and Crime*. Chicago: University of Chicago Press.

Rengert, George F., and John Wasilchick. 1985. *Suburban Burglary: A Time and Place for Everything*. Springfield, IL: Charles C. Thomas.

Roncek, D., R. Bell, and J. Francik. 1981. "Housing Projects and Crime: Testing a Proximity Hypothesis." *Social Problems 29*: 151-166.

Rose, H., and P. McCain. 1990. *Race, Place, and Risk: Black Homicide in Urban America*. Albany: State University of New York Press.

Rosenbaum, Dennis P. (1986). "The Problem of Crime Control." In D.P. Rosenbaum (ed.) *Community Crime Prevention: Does It Work?* (Pp. 11-18) Beverly Hills, CA: Sage.

Sampson, Robert J.

1985. "Neighborhood and Crime: The Structural Determinants of Personal Victimization." *Journal of Research in Crime and Delinquency 22*: 7-40.

1986a. "Neighborhood Family Structure and the Risk of Criminal Victimization." In J. Byrne and Robert Sampson (eds.) *The Social Ecology of Crime* (pp. 25-46). New York: Springer-Verlag.

1986b. "Effects of Socioeconomic Context on Official Reaction to Juvenile Delinquency." *American Sociological Review 51*: 876-885.

1987. "Communities and Crime." Pp. 91-114 in *Positive Criminology*, edited by Michael R. Gottfredson and Travis Hirschi. Beverly Hills, CA: Sage.

1988. ""Local Friendship Ties and Community Attachment in Mass Society: A Multilevel Systemic Model." *American Sociological Review 53*: 766-779.

1990. "Crime and Deviance over the Life Course: The Salience of Adult Social Bonds." *American Sociological Review 55*: 609-627.

1992. "Family Management and Child Development: Insights from Social Disorganization Theory." In Joan McCord (ed.) *Fact, Frameworks, and Forecasts: Advances in Criminological Theory, Vol. 3.* (pp. 63-93) New Brunswick, NJ: Transaction.

1997. "The Embeddedness of Child and Adolescent Development: A Community-Level Perspective on Urban Violence." In Joan McCord (ed.) *Violence and Childhood in the Inner City.* Cambridge: Cambridge University Press.

Sampson, Robert J., and W. Byron Groves. 1989. "Community Structure and Crime: Testing Social Disorganization Theory." *American Journal of Sociology 94*: 774-802.

Sampson, Robert J. and Janet L. Lauritsen. 1994. "Violent Victimization and Offending: Individual, Situational, and Community-Level Risk Factors." In Albert J. Reiss, Jr. And Jeffrey A. Roth (eds.) *Understanding and Preventing Violence: Social Influences,* Vol. 3 (pp. 1-114). Washington, D.C.: National Academy Press.

Schuerman, L., and S. Kobrin. 1986. "Community Careers in Crime."
    In Albert J. Reiss, Jr., and Michael Tonry (eds.) *Communities and
    Crime* (pp. 67-100). Chicago: University of Chicago Press.

Shaw, Clifford R. 1931. *The Natural History of a Delinquent Career*.
    Chicago: University of Chicago Press.

Shaw, Clifford R. and Henry D. McKay.

1942. *Juvenile Delinquency and Urban Areas*. Chicago: University of
    Chicago Press.

1969. *Juvenile Delinquency and Urban Areas*. (2nd Edition) Chicago:
    University of Chicago Press.

1972. *Juvenile Delinquency and Urban Areas*. (3rd Edition) Chicago:
    University of Chicago Press.

Short, James F. 1972. "Introduction to Revised Edition." In *Juvenile
    Delinquency and Urban Areas* (3rd Edition), edited by C.R. Shaw
    and H.D. McKay. Chicago: University of Chicago Press.

Shotland, R.L., and L.I. Goldstein. 1984. "The Role of Bystanders in
    Crime Control." *Journal of Social Issues 40*: 9-26.

Simcha-Fagan, O., and J. Schwartz. 1986. "Neighborhood and
    Delinquency: An Assessment of Contextual Effects." *Criminology
    24*: 667-704.

Skogan, Wesley G. and Michael G. Maxfield. 1981. *Coping with
    Crime*. Beverly Hills. Sage.

Skogan, Wesley G. 1986. "Fear of Crime and Neighborhood Change."
    Pp. 203-229 in *Communities and Crime*, edited by Albert J. Reiss,
    Jr., and Michael Tonry. Chicago: University of Chicago Press.

Skogan, Wesley G. 1990. *Disorder and Decline: Crime and the Spiral
    of Decay in American Neighborhoods*. New York: Free Press.

Slovak, Jeffrey S. 1987. "Police Organization and Policing
    Environment: Case Study of a Disjuncture." *Sociological Focus
    20*: 77-94.

Smith, Douglas R. 1986. "The Neighborhood Context of Police
    Behavior." In Albert J. Reiss, Jr., and Michael Tonry (eds.)
    Communities and Crime (pp. 313-341). Chicago: University of
    Chicago Press.

Smith, L.N., and G.D. Hill. 1991. "Victimization and Fear of Crime."
    Criminal Justice and Behavior 18: 217-239.

Smith, Douglas R., and G. Roger Jarjoura. 1988. "Social Structure and Criminal Victimization." *Journal of Research in Crime and Delinquency 25*: 27-52.

Stark, Rodney. 1996. "Deviant Places: A Theory of the Ecology of Crime." In Peter Cordella and Larry Siegal (eds.) *Readings in Contemporary Criminological Theory* (pp. 128-142). Boston: Northeastern University Press.

Suttles, Gerald D. 1968. *The Social Order of the Slum.* Chicago: University of Chicago Press.

Taub, Richard D., D. Garth Taylor, and Jan D. Dunham. 1981. "Neighborhoods and Safety." Pp. 103-119 in *Reactions to Crime,* edited by Dan A. Lewis. Beverly Hills, CA: Sage.

Taylor, Ralph B. 1998. Crime Changes in Baltimore, 1970-1994 [Computer File]. ICPSR version. Baltimore, MD: Battelle/Survey Research Associates, Inc. [producer], 1994. Ann Arbor, MI: Inter-university Consortium for Political and Social Research [distributor].

Taylor, Ralph B., Sidney Brower, and Whit Drain. 1979. *A Map of Baltimore Neighborhoods.* John Hopkins University. Baltimore, MD: Center for Metropolitan Planning and Research.

Taylor, Ralph B., and Jeanette Covington. 1988. "Neighborhood Change in Ecology and Violence." *Criminology 26*: 553-590.

Taylor, Ralph B., Stephen D. Gottfredson, and Sidney Brower. 1984. "Block Crime and Fear: Defensible Space, Local Social Ties, and Territorial Functioning." *Journal of Research in Crime and Delinquency 21*: 303-31.

Taylor, Ralph B. and Margaret Hale, 1986. "Testing Alternative Models of Fear of Crime." *Journal of Criminal Law and Criminology 77*: 151-89.

Taylor, Ralph B. and S.A. Schumaker. 1990. "Local Crime as a Natural Hazard: Implications for Understanding the Relationship Between Disorder and Fear of Crime." *American Journal of Community Psychology 18*: 619-42.

Taylor, Ralph B., S.A. Schumaker, and Stephen D. Gottfredson. 1985. "Neighborhood-Level Links between Physical Features and Local Sentiments: Deterioration, Fear, Crime, and Confidence." *Journal of Architectural Planning Research 2*: 261-275.

"The Economic Crisis of Urban America." May 18, 1992. *Business Week*, p. 38-47.

Tyler, Tom R. 1984. "Assessing the Risk of Crime Victimization: The Integration of Personal Victimization Experiences and Socially Transmitted Information." *Journal of Social Issues 40*: 27-38.

Vold, George B., Bernard, Thomas J. and Snipes, Jeffrey B. 1998. *Theoretical Criminology*, (4th Edition). Oxford: Oxford University Press.

Warr, Mark and Mark C. Stafford. 1983. "Fear of Victimization: A Look at the Proximate Causes." *Social Forces 61*: 1033-1043.

"What We Can Do Now." June 1, 1992. *Fortune*, p. 40-48.

Whyte, William F. 1981. *Street Corner Society*, 3rd ed. Chicago: University of Chicago Press.

Wilson, James Q., and George W. Kelling. 1982. "Broken Windows." *Atlantic Monthly,* March: 29-38.

Wilson, William Julius. 1987. *The Truly Disadvantaged: The Inner City, the Underclass, and Public Policy*. University of Chicago Press.

Index